19267   PS
2638
·P3

Parks

Edgar Allan Poe as literary critic

Date Due

JAN 3 '86	DEC 11 '67	OC 22 '71	
JAN 19 '66	MAR 5 '68	DE 6 '72	MAR 06 '86
MAR 22 '66	NOV 18 '68	JA 31 '73	NOV 30 1992
APR 19 '66	FE 6 '69	NO 7 '73	OCT 8 1998
MAR 9 '67	FE 27 '69	MY 7 '74	
MAY 8	NO 16 '69	NOV 20	JUL 14 1994
AUG 1 '67	AG 14 '70	DEC 2 '7	MAY 8 '95
	DE 9 '70	OCT 27 '82	OCT 7 '96
OCT 26 '67	MR 17 '71	FEB 4 '83	DEC 01 1997
	MY 17 '71	MAY 29 1990	OCT 31 2001
NOV 7 '67		OCT 23 1992	

EDGAR ALLAN POE
AS LITERARY CRITIC

EDGAR ALLAN POE

AS

LITERARY CRITIC

EDD WINFIELD PARKS

EUGENIA DOROTHY BLOUNT LAMAR
MEMORIAL LECTURES

Delivered at Mercer University on
February 11 and 12, 1964

UNIVERSITY OF GEORGIA PRESS

ATHENS

COPYRIGHT

1 9 6 4

UNIVERSITY OF GEORGIA PRESS

Library of Congress Catalog Card Number: 64-25841

Printed in the United States of America

FOOTE AND DAVIES, ATLANTA

To
Ralph H. Stephens
and
Ben W. Griffith

Contents

Contents

Foreword

THE PHRASE "ADOPTED SOUTHERNER" CAN BE USED NOWHERE more appropriately than in the case of Edgar Allan Poe, who was born in Boston of wandering theatrical parents and who later became the ward of a Richmond family. It was fortunate for the cause of Southern letters that Elizabeth Arnold Poe brought her infant son below the Mason-Dixon line, thereby giving the region its first major literary figure. Mrs. Poe's migration southward also made it possible for the Lamar Lecture Committee to invite Professor Edd Winfield Parks to deliver a series of lectures on "Poe As Literary Critic."

The speaker and subject were ideally suited. Perhaps it was the public image of Poe as the mysterious and enigmatic author of "The Raven" that drew the large audience to Mercer University's Willingham Chapel initially, but it was Dr. Parks's abilities as a platform lecturer, his skill as a writer, and his sound scholarship that kept attendance at a record high throughout the series. Dr. Parks has a varied background as a Fulbright lecturer in many parts of the world and as the author of a significant number of scholarly books and articles as well as novels and poetry; his graciousness in giving of himself to faculty and students alike made his visit to Mercer University a memorable one.

With the publication of this seventh series of Eugenia Dorothy Blount Lamar Memorial Lectures, the Lamar Lecture Committee and Mercer University reaffirm their gratitude to the late Mrs. Lamar's wisdom and generosity in endowing this perpetual series of lectures. Mrs. Lamar, a cultural leader in Macon and the South for nearly three-quarters of a century, was keenly interested in the continuation of traditional Southern values amid the kaleidoscope of social and economic changes taking place in the modern South. She left a legacy to Mercer University with the request that it be used "to provide lectures of the very highest type of scholarship which will aid in the permanent preservation of the values of Southern culture, history, and literature."

BENJAMIN W. GRIFFITH, JR., *Chairman*
The Lamar Lecture Committee

Mercer University
Macon, Georgia

Preface

IN ITS ORIGINAL FORM, THE MATERIAL IN THIS BOOK WAS
presented as the Lamar Lectures at Mercer University in
February, 1964. I have adhered to that form, but I am indebted to President Rufus C. Harris and to Professor Ben
W. Griffith, Chairman of the Lamar Lecture Committee,
for permission to expand the work considerably, with the
addition of introductory and concluding material and
buttressing notes. I am also grateful to the faculty and
students of Mercer and the people of Macon for the cordial
reception they gave to me and my wife, and to the lectures.

I have dealt almost entirely with trying to define Poe's
critical position in terms of his own writing. It is my belief that Poe developed a fairly rounded aesthetic, but
since he did this through the media of scattered magazine
reviews and articles, he has sometimes been described as a
critic who merely shaped his literary theory to fit his own
practice. I have tried to order and present evidence to the
contrary. At the same time, this does not seem to contradict
T. S. Eliot's discerning observation, in "The Music of
Poetry," that "the critical writings of poets, of which in
the past there have been some very distinguished examples,
owe a great deal of their interest to the fact that at the
back of the poet's mind, if not as his ostensible purpose,
he is always trying to defend the kind of poetry he is writ-

ing, or to formulate the kind that he wants to write." I have also tried to make this volume a companion to my *Ante-Bellum Southern Literary Critics* (1962), thus rounding out the survey of criticism in the Old South.

The research and writing have been greatly expedited by assistance from the Research Fund of the University of Georgia, through Deans Gerald B. Huff and Robert A. McRorie, and the constant assistance of W. Porter Kellam, John Marshall, Christine Burroughs, and others of the University of Georgia Library. Two colleagues, John Olin Eidson and Rayburn Moore, and my friend Jay B. Hubbell of Duke University unselfishly read the typescript and made penetrating suggestions from which I have profited. Most of all, for constant perceptive help, I am grateful to my wife, Aileen Wells Parks.

EDD WINFIELD PARKS

The University of Georgia
Athens, Georgia

Introduction

EDGAR ALLAN POE WAS THE FIRST IMPORTANT CRITIC TO
develop and to refine his critical theories through the
media of book reviews and magazine articles. Despite the
commonly-held idea that he lived "out of space, out of
time," Poe's reputation in his own day was mainly established by his reviews of contemporary books; he referred
to himself as "essentially a magazinist"; his chief ambition
was to own and edit a magazine that would publish, along
with stories, poems, and general articles, an "absolutely
independent criticism." At a time when many writers
thought that magazines were exerting a harmful influence
on literature, Poe consistently defended them:

The increase, within a few years, of the magazine literature
is by no means to be regarded as indicating what some critics
would suppose it to indicate—a downward tendency in American taste or in American letters. It is but a sign of the times—
an indication of an era in which men are forced upon the curt,
the condensed, the well-digested—in place of the voluminous.
. . . I will not be sure that men at present think more profoundly than half a century ago, but beyond question they
think with more rapidity, with more skill, with more tact,
with more of method, and less of excrescence in the thought.
Besides all this, they have a vast increase in the thinking material. They have more facts, more to think about. For this

reason, they are disposed to put the greatest amount of thought in the smallest compass.[1]

His innate liking for a literature suitable for magazine publication is one key to Poe's critical theory. A second one, which fitted hand-in-glove with the first, was his search for an ideal unity in literature, similar to the perfect unity of the universe. The natural world, it seemed to him, is governed by a divine system of adaptation in which the beginning leads inevitably to the end, in which means are exactly proportioned to the task to be accomplished, and in which the force expended is precisely proportioned to the work to be done. He sought for the same perfection of form and design in literature, in his own creative work and in the work of others. This desire for a perfect wholeness motivated his dislike for the didactic element in literature: the whole story or poem should be the communication between writer and reader; if the work were rightly done, the effect would be properly secured by the total work, and not by underlining its message or its conclusion.

Poe's old-fashioned use of one word tends to mislead modern readers. He speaks constantly of *plot* and writes many times, with only slight variation and with consistent use of the key word, that "a plot is perfect only inasmuch as we shall find ourselves unable to detach from it or disarrange any single incident involved, without ruin to the whole." Today we are suspicious of plot because it seems to arrange life too artificially. But in our critical thinking we have narrowed the term which Poe so frequently employed. He thought of it as the design, and he saw an analogy between it and the natural world. He desired a whole hamoniously complete in all its parts, a miniature universe which would be comparable to the real universe in which the beginning, middle, and end were held together by an exact and mathematically conceived unity. In the ideal literary design, the end was inevitably foreshadowed and fixed by the beginning; incidents, as middle or means, had to be precisely adjusted to the desired end.²

Poe found few books that fitted his stringent theories. As a working critic, he praised many books that only partially achieved what he ideally demanded. But he had a consistent critical theory by which to judge books, although his criteria changed somewhat as he developed. He began in 1831 by placing almost all the creative and the critical faculty in the imagination; by 1835, when he began reviewing books regularly for the *Southern Literary Messenger*,³ he was convinced that reason was equally important, and he made an intensive study of the interplay of reason and imagination. He gradually worked out a theory that imagination or inspiration represented the poetic sentiment, which he also described by such terms as poesy, ideality, and the sense of the sublime. But the poem was the means by which a poet brought to the reader a sense of the beautiful, a sense of exaltation; and the completed poem was a product of the reason.

The final stage in his critical development reveals Poe's insistence on the equality of the two forces. With imagination and with reason, "both alike infinite and both alike indestructible," the poet could create a completely unified work if each co-operating faculty exactly equalled the other. This blending of powers he described usually by the term "combining"; he also referred to it as the poetic intellect and the analytic imagination. A poet who lacked this combining force could not possibly produce a unified work.

It was a high, possibly an inhuman, ideal which Poe constantly softened and qualified in his judgments of older and of contemporary poets. He praised Andrew Marvell for achieving it, and praised Longfellow mildly for having partially achieved that goal. His highest praise, significantly, went to Nathaniel Hawthorne for his successful blending of imagination and reason in the field of the short story. Hawthorne had secured unity of effect, totality of impression, intensity, and a sense of ultimate truth in his tales. At his best, he had welded content and form into a perfect whole. Few other writers had succeeded in doing this—so few, in Poe's judgment, that to his contemporaries he seemed to deserve the title of the "tomahawk critic." Yet he seems to have erred more frequently on the side of kindness than of harshness.

He was willing to admit that the building up of a harmonious whole, in prose or in verse, was exceedingly difficult. Not many men could achieve the ultimate function of poetry: the rhythmical creation of beauty. That required a sense of physical or earthly beauty, a sense of spiritual beauty, and a sense of the suggestive power of music. Neither writer nor reader could long sustain the intensity and exaltation of supernal beauty. If the poet is to convey a unified impression of a haunting, indefinite, perfect beauty, he must severely restrict the length of his poem. If the prose writer is to secure a more factual but equally unified sense of reality, he also must limit the scope of his work.

It has been noted frequently that Poe's critical theories and his creative talents complement each other with amazing exactitude. Some later scholars have attempted to prove that the theories are only rationalizations of Poe's own creative limitations. This is undoubtedly true to the extent that he believed an author should be fully aware of the capabilities of the art that he practiced: in his own work and in his judgment of others, he held firmly to his central conception that art was not a spontaneous overflow of genius, but a designed effect.

The literary field that Poe tilled was undeniably narrow. He lacked breadth of vision, broad human sympathy, and a warmhearted comprehension of many diverse types of people. For these he substituted intensity of thought and emotion, and a tight perfection of form. His theories likewise unduly narrow the field of literature, especially of poetry. He would rule out of that domain the major works of writers like Dante, Milton, and Goethe. But his positive accomplishments were definite, and widely influential. Nowhere were they more far-reaching than in the field of criticism. At a time when romantic writers were talking of self-expression, he concentrated not on the artist but on the created work of art. It was from Poe's logical formulas for a poem that Baudelaire and the French symbolists (especially Mallarmé and, much later, Valéry) derived their form, their doctrine of the interpenetration of the senses, and their idea of an allusive, indefinite imagery and rhythm that would have the suggestiveness of music. It was from Poe's essays on form (especially "The Poetic Principle" and "The Philosophy of Composition") that Gautier and the Parnassians derived much of their philosophy that the form creates the idea.[4]

Poe's final value as a critic can hardly be judged apart from his influence on the French poets, and it was through them that he has influenced such modern American poets as T. S. Eliot and Wallace Stevens. To his contemporaries and to the immediately following generations in America, he seemed in this respect outside the main currents of American thought. But if this influence has come back to us indirectly, through Europe, another phase of his critical work had and continues to have a direct bearing on our thought. He emphasized compression, brevity, unity of effect; he set the highest value on literary types more suitable for magazines than for books. More than any other critic, Poe developed a tenable aesthetic for a magazine age.

LECTURE

ONE

Poe As a Magazine Critic

INSOFAR AS THIS BOOK CAN BE SAID TO HAVE A THESIS, IT is that Poe's critical theories were mainly formed by his work as magazine editor and critic. Before he started writing for the *Southern Literary Messenger,* he had published only one identifiable straightforward piece of literary criticism, although Floyd Stovall has argued persuasively that a major theme in the poem "Al Aaraaf" is Poe's allegorical statement of his theory of poetry. The inhabitants of this imaginary planet are without passion, without knowledge of good and evil. They are lovers of beauty, and Al Aaraaf is the birthplace of the concept of pure beauty. They are neither scientific nor didactic. Instead of knowledge, they depend on the imagination for aesthetic insight. This foreshadows, although somewhat vaguely and obscurely, Poe's belief that beauty should be the sole province of poetry.[1]

His formal criticism began with the letter which he used as a preface to his 1831 *Poems.* Although it deals almost entirely with poetry, the letter contains in embryonic forms certain general principles that Poe was to develop and to modify in his later writings. The most important of these are his attack on didacticism and his placing importance on the imagination at the expense of the reason. Poetry was "all that is airy and fairy-like"; it had for "its object an *indefinite* instead of a *definite* pleasure"; it was essentially lyrical in its character. Also, there is the note of personal ridicule (here directed against William Wordsworth and Samuel Johnson) that was occasionally to mar and in a degree to vitiate his reviews. He revealed an indebtedness to Coleridge and A. W. von Schlegel, who were to remain his chief critical mentors.

He noticed in passing that an American author had to compete against the world, and that too often readers felt that books, like their authors, improved with travel. By 1836 he had fully developed his critical theory on this point; except when personal feelings prevailed over his critical judgment, he was to adhere to this belief throughout his life. Poe believed that what we needed was an international standard of criticism. As a people we had alternated between superiority and inferiority. Yet it was equally bad to over-praise or to damn a book because it was by an American, or because it was by an Englishman. Certain American editors and readers continued to feel that an American book could be worth reading only after "repeated assurances from England that such productions were not altogether contemptible." But the intellectual atmosphere had largely changed, until now we "throw off, with the most presumptuous and unmeaning hauteur, *all* deference whatever to foreign opinion . . . and thus often find ourselves involved in the gross paradox of liking a stupid book the better, because, sure enough, its stupidity is American." This attitude seemed to Poe even more dangerous than subservience, and as editor he set himself sternly against "a current so disastrously undermining the health and prosperity of our literature."[2]

In 1831, when he was putting practically all the emphasis on the imagination, Poe had protested that "Against the subtleties which would make poetry a study —not a passion—it becomes the metaphysician to reason— but the poet to protest." By 1836, this concept had been modified. There seem to have been several related yet separate reasons. Margaret Alterton has presented detailed evidence that Poe during this period came under the tutelage first of William Wirt and then of John Pendleton Kennedy—both distinguished lawyers as well as writers. Wirt in particular was suspicious of too much imagination, and was a strong advocate of logical thought. In 1829 he had read "Al Aaraaf" before it was published and had been puzzled by it, although he thought it might please "modern readers: he steadily advised young would-be lawyers who were studying with him to cultivate severe logic and closeness of thought." One road to this was by reading carefully the essays of Edmund Burke and the legal arguments of Poe's Richmond acquaintance, Chief Justice John Marshall; another was by teaching oneself to speak and write clearly, distinctly, and to the point. Kennedy also played a part in curbing Poe's reliance on the imagination alone. Poe's greatest fault was his love of the extravagant, his fondness for the bizarre; he was "highly imaginative and a little *terrific*," added Kennedy, "but I have turned him to drudging upon whatever may make money." More important, Kennedy secured for Poe the position of Assistant Editor of the *Southern Literary Messenger* in 1835, and, before the end of the year, Editor.[3]

A second reason for the modification in his point of view was that in this period Poe had read and studied the files of foreign magazines, especially *Blackwood's*. He testifies himself to "poring over foreign files." He found in

a *Blackwood's* critique of a very bad epic poem a justification for personal ridicule; the author was right in concentrating his witticisms on the poet rather than on the poem.
Here levity seemed indispensable, for to have treated the
work seriously "would have defeated the ends of the critic,
in weakening his own authority by making himself ridiculous." He also decided that too many British critics used
the book supposedly under review as the springboard for
an independent article on the subject; even though the
article might be excellent, this was not the proper function of criticism. Moreover, the British critics tended to be
arrogant, and some, like Christopher North, extravagant
in praise or blame; but they were attempting a judicial
criticism founded on literary standards. The *Blackwood's*
coterie leaned rather heavily on A. W. and Frederick von
Schlegel's theories, but Poe was in full agreement with
many of their ideas. Although he so changed and developed the concepts that they became his own, Poe may
have found in Schlegel's dictum that poetry is "the power
of creating what is beautiful" the germ of his own definition of poetry as the rhythmical creation of beauty; in
Schlegel's more limited idea that the "essence of the north-
ern poetry" is melancholy his own belief that melancholy
is "the most legitimate of all the poetical tones"; he undoubtedly got from Schlegel and Coleridge his embryonic
concept of the principle of unity or totality of effect.[4]

It is quite possible that he had already been introduced
to these critical ideas at the University of Virginia, in
1826. George Tucker, Professor of Moral Philosophy and
a leading proponent of the Scottish school of common-
sense philosophy, delivered many lectures on literary
theory. Tucker distinguished between the "soul" of poetry,
which he found in the "perception of the beautiful and the
grand," and the poem itself, through which, in R. C. Mc-
Lean's words, "The poet conveys a sense of the beautiful

and sublime to his readers, using carefully ordered, musical language." He thought that great poetry must transcend realism, and that to some degree it achieved this by approximating music. Tucker also agreed with Coleridge that the aim of poetry is pure pleasure, and he drew upon Archibald Alison to indicate the necessity for "unity of emotion," in a poem or a tale. In the latter, Tucker argued likewise that the horrible could be combined with the beautiful.

These are suggestive ideas that may have been germinal in Poe's development. But Poe did not take any of Tucker's classes and may not have attended any of Tucker's lectures or read any of his essays; and he knew at first hand Hugh Blair's *Lectures on Rhetoric and Belles-Lettres,* Lord Kames's *Elements of Criticism,* the critical writings of Archibald Alison, Thomas Reid, and especially Dugald Stewart, as well as the works of the English John Locke and the Irish Edmund Burke. Poe had the magazinist's gift of ready assimilation. But he had also read widely in the British reviews, and had absorbed many of the ideas of the reviewers. All these were part and parcel of the intellectual life at the University of Virginia, and Robert D. Jacobs has persuasively indicated that Poe's critical theories had their origin in Jefferson's Virginia. This is undoubtedly true in part, but there is too little exact information for it to be conclusive. Unfortunately, although perhaps appropriately considering the subject-matter, we must fall back upon the old Scottish verdict, "not proven."[5]

Poe brought, then, to the *Southern Literary Messenger* certain basic yet embryonic ideas on criticism. He began mildly enough with a graceful if hastily-written tribute to *Horse-Shoe Robinson,* by his friend John Pendleton Kennedy. But he seems already to have felt that for a magazine to be successful it must "kick up a dust," and he found the perfect target for his tornado in a rather silly, badly-written novel by a well-known New York journalist, Theodore Fay. The novel, *Norman Leslie,* had received what Poe considered inordinate praise and puffery before it was published, and he used every weapon in his arsenal to attack it, from personal ridicule to merciless analysis. Reviews of this nature were to earn for him the unceasing enmity of most of the New York literati and the title of the Tomahawk Critic; they led Lowell to write that Poe sometimes mistook his phial of prussic acid for his ink well, or Dr. Thomas Holley Chivers of Georgia to protest that surgeons never cut away "so much of a *part* as to endanger the vitality of the *whole.*"

Yet Poe intended that his reviews should be fair and just. When in 1836 the Richmond *Courier* accused him of "regular cutting and slashing," he responded that the *Courier* was wrong in calling this as bad as "indiscriminate laudation. It is infinitely worse—it is horrible. The laudation may proceed from—philanthropy, if you please; but the 'indiscriminate cutting and slashing' only from the vilest passions of our nature." Since the preceding December (1835), he had reviewed 95 books in the *Messenger*. In 79 of these, commendation had greatly predominated over the few sentences of censure; in 7, praise slightly prevailed; in 5, censure greatly predominated; but only three reviews were, he felt, harshly condemnatory, and only one "unexceptionally condemned." What he had aimed at was "rigid justice and impartiality," and the reviews had been widely lauded for having attained this goal.[6]

One method of achieving impartiality was by firmly rooting generalizations in textual analysis. This extended even to such minute matters as punctuation. Kennedy's *Horse-Shoe Robinson* seemed "singularly deficient in this respect—and yet we noticed no fault of this nature in Swallow Barn. . . . It cannot be said that the point is one of no importance—it is of very great importance. A slovenly punctuation will mar, in a greater or less degree, the brightest paragraph ever penned." He was equally concerned about the use and especially the mis-use of words. He ridiculed Fay's persistent use of the word *blister*. Although Simms in *The Partisan* made a few downright mistakes, a greater error was his overuse of pet words like *coil, hug,* and *old-time;* to illustrate this, Poe quoted eight sentences using *old-time* and noted that "we believe there are ten times as many more interspersed throughout the work." Bulwer-Lytton had often and justly been charged with defects of style, but the charges had been "sadly deficient in specification"; Poe documents his own charge that Bulwer's English was often "turgid, involved, and ungrammatical" with four solidly-printed pages of examples. Bulwer had the eyes falling asleep, instead of the person; he misused simple words like *flung* and *tossed,* in an attempt to give greater intensity to his prose; he had an absolute mania for metaphor, until he could not "express a dozen consecutive sentences in an honest and manly manner." Poe objected to such absurdities as "the wind roaring in the air" and eight men who were "attired like the two first who were included in the number."[7]

Poe was convinced that he had "at all times been particularly careful not to deal in generalities, and have never, if we remember aright, advanced in any single instance an unsupported assertion." In poetry he demonstrated this almost too thoroughly in his analysis of Joseph Rodman Drake's "The Culprit Fay." The critic was engaged in proving that the poem was a product of the fancy rather than of the imagination, and that it had been over-praised by patriotic reviewers. The greater part was destitute of any imagination whatever. After determining the size and nature of his fairies, the poet had only provided "mere specifications of qualities, of habiliments, of punishments, of occupations, of circumstances" which would be appro-

priate. A fairy-warror puts on an acorn helmet with a
thistle-down plume, and a corselet that once was "the wild
bee's golden vest," and takes up a shield that once was "the
shell of a lady-bug queen." Poe quotes many other examples, but most effectively he inserts a parody to indicate
how easily this type of fanciful poetry can be written, with
different yet equally appropriate equipments: his own
bluebell helmet is "plumed with the down of the hum-
ming-bird." Poe found a few passages that evidenced the
ideality some American critics had claimed for the poem,
but he found many incongruities. One might accept a race
of fairies in the far away and long ago, but to be asked,
"in a tone of sentiment and language adapted to the loftiest
breathings of the Muse, to imagine a race of Fairies in the
vicinity of West Point" struck him as merely ridiculous.
To be told that a fairy about an inch in height had committed a deadly sin by falling in love with a mortal maiden
who might be "six feet in her stockings" was even more
ridiculous. Critics who denominated such work as imaginative had failed in their primary duty: a close reading and
logical analysis of the work being reviewed.

Some of Poe's strictures may have been harsh and even
unjust, but at least they were based on a careful examination of the material. Also, he was no longer willing, as in
the Preface to the 1831 *Poems,* to allow that imagination
was enough in itself. In the Drake-Halleck review, he
made a distinction that he was to develop, but not basically to modify: the Faculty of Ideality is the sentiment or
principle or faculty (words that he used interchangeably)
of Poesy in the larger meaning of the word. This sentiment is the sense of the beautiful, of the sublime, of the
mystical; it is the idea "of Intellectual Happiness here,
and the Hope of a higher Intellectual Happiness hereafter." But this sentiment need not be expressed in words.
It might take the form of painting, sculpture, architecture,

or landscape gardening; in words, of a tale or a poem. When this faculty of ideality was given tangible form by an artist, the area of judgment changed. The critic was not judging the degree or the intensity of the artist's feeling. Self-expression was not, as so many romantic poets and critics felt, of supreme or even of very great importance. Poe drew a sharp line of demarcation: " a poem is not the Poetic faculty, but the *means* of exciting it in mankind." It was through the controlling guidance of the artist that his imaginative concept was shaped and ordered so as to give it the greatest impact on other men; in turn, the critic or metaphysician could determine by analysis the means used to create the effect. Imagination remained supreme; without it, only secondary and relatively minor works of art could be achieved, although some of these might be pleasing and gain wide popular favor; yet reason was necessary as an aid to the imagination in producing the loftiest works of art. By September, 1836, this conjunction seemed to Poe inevitable, for "the reasoning powers never exist in perfection unless when allied with a very high degree of the imaginative faculty."[8]

By the time that he left the *Messenger* in January, 1837, Poe's critical theory and his lifetime ambition had begun to take form. His resignation was not quite voluntary. No doubt the main reason was the owner's objection to Poe's drinking and consequent lack of efficiency, but there were subsidiary reasons. White felt that Poe's stringent reviews were making enemies for the magazine, and this troubled the cautious printer; even more, that Poe's editorial standards were cramping him "in the exercise of my own judgment, as to what articles I shall or shall not admit into my work." On his part, Poe was dissatisfied. White had only monetary standards as criteria; he had no real conception either of literature or of a magazine. As Poe wrote, the drudgery was excessive, the salary contemptible. More important, he could not, since he had no proprietary interest in the magazine, impose upon it the needed individuality and character that would give distinction to a periodical. But it was "the one great purpose of my literary life" to establish and edit such a journal.[9]

Poe was unfortunate in his timing. When he left Richmond, he thought that he had firm literary commitments in New York that would at least assure his family of a comfortable living. He did not reckon on the inflation that was followed by the long-lasting Panic that began in May, 1837, with the inevitable dwindling of his literary markets. Although his novelette, *The Narrative of Arthur Gordon Pym*, was published by Harper and Brothers in 1838, the book did not sell; it was in fact described by a friend as the most unsuccessful of his works. Since he could not place enough literary work to live on and since with established magazines being temporarily or permanently discontinued it was obviously hopeless to start a new one, Poe moved to Philadelphia and soon became Associate Editor of *Burton's Gentleman's Magazine*. Once again, Poe was unhappy with the literary standards of the editor and the magazine. William Burton was more interested in acting and in establishing a repertory theater than he was in writing or editing.

Poe thought of the job as a necessary stopgap. He postponed but did not give up his idea of having a magazine of his own, in which he would "kick up a dust." His critical contributions to *Burton's* were, he wrote, in the main perfunctory, but even so it was "not pleasant to be taxed with the twaddle of other people," as was inevitable in a magazine that published anonymous reviews. As a result of this experience, Poe came to believe that publishing reviews anonymously was at once cowardly and in-

iquitous; author and reader alike were entitled to know
the name of the reviewer, and thus to evaluate the fairness
and the authority of the critique.[10]

By June, 1840, Poe had prepared a prospectus of his
new journal, the *Penn Magazine*. He wanted a first-rate
magazine, selling at five dollars instead of the customary
three, that would include the best features of current
American and British journals and that would pay con-
tributors liberally enough to secure the best literary aid
"from the highest and purest sources."[11] He noted here
and elsewhere that the lack of an international copyright
law prevented or hampered the publication of all but the
most popular native books, including novels, and books
of stories and poems more often required a subsidy than
brought in a monetary return to the author. The result
was that "Literature is at a sad discount. . . . Without an
international copyright law, American authors may as
well cut their throats." The magazine offered the one possibility of hope.[12]

Poe emphasized especially the need for "an honest and
a fearless opinion . . . an absolutely independent criticism." This would be free of the pressure of publishers
and the partisanship of cliques; it would be based on
analysis and aloof from personal bias. He felt that he had
mellowed; the critical notices in the *Messenger* had been
marked by "a somewhat overdone causticity"; those in the
Penn Magazine would "retain this trait of severity in so
much only as the calmest yet sternest sense of justice will
permit." In critical and creative writing, the standards of
judgment would be international, for the aim of the magazine would be chiefly "to *please* . . . through means of
versatility, originality, and pungency," leaving instruction
in other hands; and it would regard "the world at large
as the true audience of the author." Unfortunately, the
combination of illness, personal poverty, and national de-

pression prevented his carrying out this ambitious plan, although in April, 1841, he wrote to a friend that the *Penn Magazine* was "scotched, not killed." Since he and his family had to live, he joined the editorial staff of *Graham's Magazine*. Graham allowed Poe greater latitude than he had ever had before, and perhaps in recompense Poe wrote for the magazine the best and most significant of his critical reviews.

Even so, *Graham's* was not the magazine that he wanted to edit. It had too many non-literary departments, too many cheap illustrations, and catered too much to popular taste. For a time he had optimistic hopes that he and the proprietor could start a second magazine, and in letters to Kennedy, Longfellow, Cooper, Bryant, and other well-known authors he re-affirmed his faith in the values of magazine literature: "the tendency of the age lies in this way . . . The brief, the terse, the condensed, and the readily circulated will take the place of the diffuse, the ponderous, and the inaccessible." This was his belief, and this was a theme he was to repeat many times before he died.[13]

In the meantime, he continued to develop his critical theories through his reviews. Although he had praised Defoe's method of achieving verisimilitude, he was convinced that minuteness of detail and literal realism were not enough. To give the idea of any desired object, it was necessary to tone down or even to neglect utterly certain portions, and to highlight those portions by which the idea of the object is afforded. In his review of Dickens's *Old Curiosity Shop*, he stated this concept firmly: "No critical principle is more firmly based in reason than that a certain amount of exaggeration is essential to the proper depicting of truth itself. We do not paint an object to be true, but to appear true to the beholder." There must be no confusion between the intent of the writer and the effect on the reader: the immature poet, for example, is likely "to think himself sublime wherever he is obscure, because obscurity is a source of the sublime—thus confounding obscurity of expression with the expression of obscurity."[14]

It was this concern for the psychological impact upon the reader that led him to prefer the tale to the novel. The long book which must necessarily be read at several sittings and with distracting interruptions could never have the unity or totality of effect that the shorter work could have. The multiplicity of incidents, the jumping from one set of characters to another, and the need for elaboration rather than compression presented added difficulties. Perfection of plot was impossible in the sense in which Poe defined plot: "that in which no part can be displaced without ruin to the whole." A careful novelist might succeed in achieving the ordinarily-accepted definition, that none of the leading incidents could be removed without detriment to the whole, but the structure was too cumbersome and long-drawn-out for the artist to attain perfection, that "unattainable goal to which his eyes are always directed, but of the possibility of attaining which he still endeavours, if wise, to cheat himself into the belief."

Clearly, Poe had in mind two unities: the first imposed by the writer upon his material; the second and almost equally important, the unity felt by the reader. It was impossible for the poet to achieve totality of effect in the epic or narrative poem, or the novelist in the popular three-volume novel; it was likewise impossible for the reader to feel this totality unless he could read the poem or the story at a single sitting. This double unity could be attained only in the lyric poem which could be read in half an hour, or the prose tale which (since it required less concentration) could be read in a maximum of two hours. Significantly, these are the types of literature ideally suited for magazine publication. It was a more difficult type of writing, but the stern demands of a high art entailed great labor if the work was to have "the beauty of Unity, Totality, Truth."[15]

Could the literary critic help to establish an intellectual climate out of which great literary works could be produced? Poe was convinced that he could. One function of the critic was to point out defects and demerits in a published work; if this were properly done, the merits would be apparent. This should not be done in a captious spirit, but as a part of the unending quest for doing better what had only been well done. This meant also that the critic must know what his business was. It was his function to judge books fairly and without subservience to other critics, but it was not his function to encourage a merely national literature by praising bad books. On the contrary, the critic must keep in mind that "the world at large" was the only "proper stage for the literary *histrio.*" Likewise, he must remain independent of the dictation of publishers and the influence of coteries. Only strong and well-edited magazines would ever provide a suitable vehicle for an honest and impartial criticism.[16]

That American criticism was neither honest nor impartial seemed to him indicated by the wide discrepancy between private and public critical judgments. In conversation, critics were mainly in agreement as to the merits of individual authors, but in their public magazine comments a member of the *Knickerbocker* group invariably praised the books by members of his literary coterie, although privately he would admit or even declare them to be stupid; a Transcendentalist critic would find merit in the most obscure balderdash of a fellow-transcendentalist poet. In 1846, there was general agreement in private literary circles as to Bryant's poetical merit, but some years earlier he had been widely and indiscriminately overpraised. The new tendency was to underestimate his real if conservative literary powers. One attitude was as bad as the other. Poe admitted that it was difficult for a critic to write justly and fairly about the work of men like Bryant and Irving, for they had become national institutions during their lives. For another reason, the merits of Nathaniel Hawthorne were "scarcely recognized by the press and the public," although in private it was conceded that he "evinces extraordinary genius"; but this opinion remained a spoken and not a written one because, first, "Mr. Hawthorne is a poor man, and, secondly, that he is *not* a literary quack." Yet if ever America was to have a healthy intellectual climate, it must have through its magazines a temperate, impartial evaluation of what we had achieved as well as what needed to be done. Although of course he never fully succeeded, Poe did more than any other individual to bring about a healthier, sounder note in our literary criticism.[17]

Another dangerous quicksand was what Poe labelled "the cant of *generality*." Anonymous writers, being unknown, were more concerned to write fluently at so much a page than they were to write well. The book too often became an excuse for an independent essay. Some of these were excellent, and Poe admitted that a good essay was a good thing; but this type of writing did not fulfil the legitimate function of criticism. The reviewer should instead survey the book, give an analysis of its contents, and pass judgment on its merits and defects. This was not easy: an analysis of a book "is a matter of time and of mental exertion. For many classes of composition there is required a deliberate perusal, with notes, and subsequent generalizations." It was easier to present random comments and copious extracts, but these were not enough. Only through the difficult labor of analysis could one give a fair and reasoned critique of a book.

When Cornelius Mathews argued that criticism now had

a wider scope and a universal interest, that it now included every type of literature except the imaginative and the strictly dramatic, Poe dissented vigorously. Criticism is *not,* he asserted, "an essay, nor a sermon, nor an oration, nor a chapter in history, nor a philosophical speculation, nor a prose-poem, nor an art novel, nor a dialogue. In fact, it can be nothing in the world but—a criticism." It could not be anything or everything at once, and the attempt to make it so would reduce it to the level of farce. True, the erroneous facts and the shaky opinions of a historian or a theologian might properly be corrected by one of his peers, but this would be in his capacity as a scholar rather than a critic. But literary criticism should be limited to comment upon the art of the book. This included the small as well as the great. The conscientious reviewer could not dismiss "errors of grammar" as beneath his notice; he could not "hand over an imperfect rhyme or a false quantity to the proofreader." These were essential to its artistry. But the author as a man should not be pilloried: "A book is written—and it is only *as the book* that we subject it to review. With the opinions of the work, considered otherwise than in their relation to the work itself, the critic has really nothing to do. It is his part simply to decide upon *the mode* in which these opinions are brought to bear. . . . In this, the only true and intelligible sense, it will be seen that criticism, the test or analysis of *Art,* (*not* of opinion) is only properly employed upon productions which have their basis in art itself."[18]

As a working reviewer, Poe dealt with many books that to his mind had no basis in art: histories, books of travel, biographies, even textbooks. Some of these reviews are far from perfunctory. Thus he wrote a long appreciative article on Washington Irving's *Astoria,* and he even imbedded a cherished aesthetic principle in a travel book on England: the author had realized that the apparent, not the real, is the province of the artist, and that to give *"the idea of any desired object, the toning down, or the utter neglect of certain portions of that object is absolutely necessary to the proper bringing out of other portions— portions by whose sole instrumentality the idea of the object is afforded."* However, this was unusual. In the main, Poe reserved his discussion of critical principles for his reviews of poetry and of fiction.[19]

It is through these that the development of Poe's thought can be charted. The young poet who had put all the emphasis on the imagination shifted to the position that while the imagination was all-important in the sentiment or concept of poetry, the reason or artistry must take over in turning the sentiment into a poem, and shifted again when he decided that imagination and reason were of equal importance and must work concurrently. It is not by accident or rationalization that he declared the lyric poem (which is ideally suited for magazine publication) to be the best and perhaps the only true poetry, or that he thought the short tale the fairest field which could be afforded in the domain of prose for the exercise of genius. His rather shadowy ideas of fictional structure developed into a rounded if somewhat limited aesthetic of the short story, and even embraced the detective story. These tales of ratiocination, being something in a new key, were especially attractive to magazine readers because of their novelty and ingenuity. But the writer must learn to play fair; he must not in his own words mislead the reader.[20]

In poetry and in fiction, it was necessary that poets and story writers recognize the value of tension rather than of extension. This could be achieved only through works short enough to have totality of impression, unity of effect. Starting from the ideas of Schlegel and of Coleridge, adapting and developing these concepts to his own ends, Poe was gradually working toward a new form of literary art. Sometimes personal feelings distracted him. His desire for originality and his feeling that his own work was unduly neglected led to an obsession with the topics of originality and of plagiarism. These and other ideas he developed, hammered out, and refined through the media of book reviews. This resulted in some shifting of his critical position, but he remained remarkably consistent in his major endeavor; he was developing an aesthetic that would justify and ennoble a first-rate magazine literature.

LECTURE

TWO

Poe on Fiction

BY 1831, WHEN HE WAS TWENTY-TWO YEARS OLD, POE HAD become very much interested in the writing of short stories. Clearly in those days in Baltimore he had read and analyzed many magazine tales and sketches; he wrote parodies of several of these types that may well be considered as indirect literary criticism. The most obvious example is "A Tale of Jerusalem," since it is a burlesque of part of a trashily sentimental religious novel; the most interesting example is "Metzengerstein," which started as an imitation of the Gothic romances but in the writing gathered such momentum that it became a powerful allegory, with evil leading to its own self-destruction. Five of these stories were published in the *Philadelphia Saturday Courier* in 1832; by 1833, when his story "Ms. Found in a Bottle" won the prize offered by the *Baltimore Saturday Visiter,* Poe had written six more and had collected the eleven (later sixteen) into a unified work that he titled "Tales of the Folio Club." Each tale was to be read aloud

24

by its author, and followed by remarks of the group on each. Poe specifically stated that "These remarks are intended as a burlesque on criticism." Unfortunately, all the critical commentaries have been lost, so that we can only infer that Poe had been studying the English and American magazine criticism as closely as the fiction.[1]

When early in 1835 Poe began reviewing regularly for the *Southern Literary Messenger,* he discovered that he must deal with novels more often than with stories, for the simple reason that novels were more popular and therefore more readily publishable. Although Poe was willing to praise individual works highly, he did not like the form. In particular, he was dubious about the historical romance, since it was not a self-contained work: "The interweaving of fact with fiction is at all times hazardous, and presupposes on the part of general readers that degree of intimate acquaintance with fact which should never be presupposed. In the present instance, the author has failed, so we think, in confining either his truth or his fable within its legitimate individual domain. Nor do we at all wonder at his failure in performing what no novelist whatever has hitherto performed."

His other doubts about the novel as an art-form developed gradually. Yet in what seems to have been his first review of a novel (Robert Montgomery Bird's *Calavar: A Romance of Mexico,* Feb. 1835), he objected to a certain awkwardness in the invention and arrangement of the story, and objected also that the miraculous agencies employed by the author are "too *unnatural* even for romance." In a brief upsurge of national pride, he proclaimed it "an American production, which will not shrink from competition with the very best European works of the same character," and surpassed by only one or two of James Fenimore Cooper's. Yet he qualified his praise carefully. It was a good work "if boldness of design, vigor of thought, copiousness and power of language,—thrilling incident, and graphic and magnificent description, can make a good novel." When he reviewed Bird's sequel, *The Infidel,* however, Poe complained of a lack of unity in the design. The author hurried from delineating one incident of slaughter and violence to another; he left himself insufficient time for characterization.

Both novels are set in Mexico, at the time of the Spanish conquest. It is worth noting that Poe did not cavil at remoteness of scene, either geographically or historically. Many contemporary critics did, but Poe in fact preferred remoteness. Perhaps as a result, Bird set his next novel, *The Hawks of Hawk-Hollow,* in Pennsylvania during the Revolutionary War. Although the author had the advantage of knowing the locale at first hand and worked in some dramatic incidents, Poe thought that he showed less originality than in his Mexican novels. His indebtedness to Scott was embarrassingly evident, yet there was little to remind the reader of *Ivanhoe* or *Kenilworth* or "above all with that most pure, perfect, and radiant gem of fictitious literature the *Bride of Lammermoor.*" Although a few characters were well-drawn, most of them were inconsistent and some even contradictory. If by style the reader meant only the prose, then in general it was faultless; if however by style one meant "the prevailing tone and manner which give character and individuality," Dr. Bird had been less fortunate, for the book had been "composed with great inequality of manner—at times forcible and manly—at times sinking into the merest childishness and imbecility." Regretfully, Poe judged that it had "no pretensions to *originality* of manner, or of style."[2]

When he was confronted in 1836 with *Sheppard Lee,* he did not connect it with Bird. After wryly noting that the book is an original and that its "deviations, however indecisive, from the more beaten paths of imitation, look well for our future literary prospects," Poe outlines for the reader the seven different types of metempsychosis that the protagonist undergoes. Although he writes favorably of "some very excellent chapters on abolition" after Lee has become Nigger Tom, Poe shows relatively little interest in the satire on contemporary social and political conditions. But the fictional idea and the form roused him to critical speculation.

Poe objects even to the possibility (accepted by the sister but not fully shared by Lee) that the transmigrations might have occurred only in delirium, brought on by an accident. This was to trifle with the reader. There were two general methods of telling such stories, and the author had selected the poorer one: "He conceives his hero endowed with some idiosyncrasy beyond the common lot of human nature, and thus introduces him to a series of adventure which, under ordinary circumstances, could occur only to a plurality of persons." But the character partly changes with each transmigration, and there is little attempt to show the influence of varied events "upon a character *unchanging.*" In fact, the narrative would be more effective if it dealt with seven different individuals.

There is a second and better way. That is for the author to avoid a jocular manner and directness of expression, and leave much to the imagination, "as if the author were firmly impressed with the truth, yet astonished at the immensity, of the wonders he relates, and for which, professedly, he neither claims nor anticipates credence. . . . The attention of the author, who does not depend upon explaining away his incredibilities, is directed to giving them the character and the luminousness of truth, and thus are brought about, unwittingly, some of the most vivid creations of human intellect."[3]

Poe had fewer reservations about the work of his friend

and mentor, John Pendleton Kennedy, although friendship did not restrain him from some sharp criticism. When he reviewed *Horse-Shoe Robinson* in May, 1835, he began with a tribute to Kennedy's earlier novel: "We have not yet forgotten, nor is it likely we shall very soon forget, the rich simplicity of diction—the manliness of tone—the admirable traits of Virginian manners, and the striking pictures of still life, to be found in *Swallow Barn*." But that book was too obviously in the manner of Addison and Irving; oddly, disregarding Scott, Cooper, and other historical romancers, Poe throught that *Horse-Shoe Robinson* deserved to be called original. The characterization was excellent, the descriptions of the Revolutionary War accurate and informative, the style at once simple and forcible, yet richly figurative and poetical. But a form that permitted the author to make the romantic hero less important than the titular hero did not fully adhere to the proprieties of fiction.

Poe uses the review for one bit of criticism on the form of the novel. Too many writers "delay as long as possible the main interest"; Kennedy with good judgment has "begun at the beginning," introducing his prominent characters and line of action immediately. He objected to Kennedy's over-use of the dash. To prove that it was "unnecessary or superfluous" in many instances, Poe quoted a paragraph as Kennedy had punctuated it and then reproduced the same passage without the dashes. He easily proved his point with this effective textual criticism.

In general, Kennedy seemed to have the eye of a painter rather than the eye of a novelist. Poe thought that each of Kennedy's three novels revealed "boldness and force of thought, (disdaining ordinary embellishment, and depending for its effect upon masses rather than details), with a predominant *sense of the picturesque* pervading and giving color to the whole." This was particularly true of *Swallow Barn,* which "is but a rich succession of picturesque still-life pieces."[4]

Poe's strictures on Bird and Kennedy had been mild enough, and the reviews on the whole favorable. Perhaps, as some later writers have suggested, he had been deliberately waiting for a well-publicized book by a prominent author that he could, in his own favorite phrase, "use up," and thus draw attention to himself and to the *Southern Literary Messenger;* more probably, he was irritated by the frenzied advance publicity and the undeserved, lavish praise that a bad novel had received. At any rate, Poe in December, 1835, published a merciless critique of Theodore S. Fay's *Norman Leslie,* and from that time on he was embroiled in the savage literary wars of the period. For Fay was an associate editor of the New York *Mirror* and a favorite of the *Knickerbocker* group.

The review may also be considered as one of Poe's earliest efforts to foster an honest American criticism. The first paragraph tends to bear this out: "This is *the* book— *the* book *par excellence*—the book bepuffed, beplastered, and be-*Mirrored*. . . . For the sake of everything puff, puffing and puffable, let us take a peep at its contents." This charge of over-puffing American books Poe was to repeat many times; although somewhat unevenly, he worked continually toward making American literary criticism more balanced and less indiscriminate. Before he proceeded, as usual, to give a lengthy summary of the plot, Poe descended into the personal ridicule that occasionally disfigures his critical work. For some reason, he objected violently to dedications, and he sneers at this one. With more point if he has in mind fiction, he asks what is the point of Prefaces in general, and of Fay's in particular.[5] When Fay explained that, although his story

was founded on fact, he had transformed certain characters, particularly that of a young lady, Poe worked in
parenthetically and unnecessarily: "oh fi! Mr. Fay—oh,
Mr. Fay, fi!" When Fay requested the "indulgence of the
solemn and sapient critics," Poe answered with more perti-
nence that *"we,* at least, are neither solemn nor sapient,
and, therefore, do not feel ourselves bound to show him a
shadow of mercy."

Poe's summary of the complex and unbelievable plot
is reasonably fair, but in his commentary he unerringly
picked those items in which Fay had overstrained, and had
achieved only a meretricious effect. The husband
threatened to leave his wife; she first beseeched him to
stay, then in turn threatened him: "It was the first un-
coiling of the basilisk within me (good Heavens, a snake
in a lady's stomach!). He gazed on me incredulously, and
coolly smiled. You remember that smile—I fainted!!!'
Alas! Mr. Davy Crockett,—Mr. Davy Crockett, alas! thou
art beaten hollow—thou art defunct, and undone! thou
hast indeed succeeded in grinning a squirrel from a tree,
but it surpassed even thine extraordinary abilities to smile
a lady into a fainting fit."

This "Tale of the Present Times" he roundly pro-
nounced to be "the most inestimable piece of balderdash
with which the common sense of the good people of
America was ever so openly or so villainously insulted."[6]

Poe's lowest descent into personalities, in his *SLM* reviews, seems uncalled for. Fay had been unduly puffed
and praised; he had written a bad novel. William Gilmore Simms belonged to no clique; he had received only
a modicum of praise; he had written some powerful if
extremely uneven novels, among them *The Partisan.* Poe
listed several of these works, although not indicating
whether or not he had read any of them, before getting
to the dedication. It is a brief and simple inscription of

thirty-three words, to a close friend. It is impossible to see what in it could have infuriated Poe. He objected to the brevity and terseness of the dedication, and imagined the author calling on Richard Yeadon to present him with a copy of *The Partisan*. Poe tortured each word to wrench some unpleasant connotation from it and ascribed this feeling to Yeadon, until at the end he has that worthy "kick the author of 'The Yemassee' downstairs." In fact, Yeadon was flattered by the dedication, as any friend might well have been; there was no factual basis for the vicious burlesque. This was Poe at his nastiest, but the tone of the entire review is little better.

After his usual summary, including his customary fling at the woodenness of the romantic hero, Poe noted that some of the characters are excellent, some horrible: the historical ones well-drawn, the fictional ones hardly credible. He objected to Porgy as "an insufferable bore" and as "a backwoods imitation of Sir Somebody Guloseton, the epicure, in one of the Pelham novels." It is not surprising that Poe found nothing humorous in the character of Porgy, but his condemnation of the soldier's mild oaths seems excessive, especially when he lists a considerable number for the benefit of readers, with the excuse that "such attempts to render profanity less despicable by rendering it amusing, should be frowned down indignantly by the public." With more justice Poe objected to Simms's hasty and slipshod writing, though it hardly merits the statement that Simms's "English is bad—shockingly bad." Indeed, Poe's examples reveal as much about his own idiosyncrasies as about Simms's ignorance—but at least the critic documented his charge with numerous examples.

The author of "Berenice" objected, also, to Simms's use of the horrible in realistically describing floggings and murders. He did not object to Simms's manufacturing his own chapter epigraphs: they are "quite as convenient as the extracted mottoes of his contemporaries. All, we think, are abominable."

Poe had found little that was good in *The Partisan,* but at the end of the review he attempted to modify his earlier sweeping judgments. It was "no ordinary work. Its historical details are replete with interest. The concluding scenes are well drawn. Some passages descriptive of swamp scenery are exquisite. Mr. Simms has evidently the eye of a painter. Perhaps, in sober truth, he would succeed better in sketching a landscape than he has done in writing a novel."[7]

In his review of *The Damsel of Darien,* Poe changed his tone entirely. Simms was worthy of being treated with respect; of his earlier works, *Martin Faber* "well deserves a permanent success," and even *The Partisan* was allowed to have "many excellences," along with "very many disfiguring features." *The Damsel* he thought a "much better book; evincing stricter study and care, with a far riper judgment, and a more rigidly disciplined fancy." This story of the dreams, adventures, and explorations of Vasco Nuñez de Balboa had little plot and adhered too closely to historical fact, but it had many "fine episodical pieces interspersed throughout the book." Yet the "most really meritorious" part of the book was the ballad, "Indian Serenade"—a precursor of Poe's later, more generalized statement that "as a poet, indeed, we like him far better than as a novelist."

It is not surprising, in fact, that the works he praised most highly are novelettes rather than novels, concentrating on psychology rather than on action, or that he reserved his highest praise for Simms's short stories in *The Wigwam and the Cabin.* As tales, each was excellent; together they illustrated the border history of the South. "Grayling, or Murder Will Out" was the best: "We have no hesitation in calling it the best ghost-story we have ever read. It is full of the richest and most vigorous imagination—is forcibly conceived—and detailed throughout with a degree of artistic skill which has had no parallel among American storytellers since the epoch of Brockden Brown."[8]

Poe's admiration for James Fenimore Cooper was decidedly limited. True, he solicited contributions for the *Southern Literary Messenger* and the projected *Penn Magazine,* and he was willing (as in the case of Irving, Paulding, Bryant, Halleck, and Catharine M. Sedgwick) to "make reasonable allowance in estimating the absolute merit of our literary pioneers." He divided writers of fiction into two classes: "a popular and widely circulated class read with pleasure but without admiration—in which the author is lost or forgotten; or remembered, if at all, with something very nearly akin to contempt; and then, a class not so popular, nor so widely diffused, in which, at every paragraph, arises a distinctive and highly pleasurable interest, springing from our perception and appreciation of the skill employed, or the genius evinced in the composition. After perusal of the one class, we think solely of the book—after reading the other, chiefly of the author. The former class leads to popularity—the latter to fame. In the former case, the books sometimes live, while the authors usually die; in the latter, even when the works perish, the man survives. Among American writers of the less circulated, but more worthy and artistical fictions, we may mention Mr. Brockden Brown, Mr. John Neal, Mr. Simms, Mr. Hawthorne; at the head of the more popular division we may place Mr. Cooper."

It is difficult to understand on what basis Poe compiled the first list. Hawthorne assuredly belongs on it; John Neal assuredly does not. Brown's Gothicism appealed to Poe's taste, and presumably it was this element in a few of

Simms's novels that caused him to be included, although
the same criteria that disqualified Cooper would seem also
to disqualify Simms. The distinction once made, however,
Poe was willing to allow Cooper some positive merits,
along with some glaring defects. He defended Cooper's
right to attack the bull-headed prejudices of his own
countrymen: "Since it is the fashion to decry the author
of 'The Prairie' just now, we are astonished at no degree
of malignity or scurrility whatever on the part of the
little gentlemen who are determined to follow that fashion." Cooper had never been known to fail, either in the
forest or on the sea, although sometimes his success has
little to do with the values of fiction. In reviewing *Mer-
cedes of Castile,* Poe started off roundly: "As a history,
this work is invaluable; as a novel, it is well nigh worthless"—in fact, the "worst *novel* ever penned by Mr. Cooper."

In general, characterization was not Cooper's forte.
Neither was plot, of which he seemed "altogether regardless or incapable." In a novel, this was not a fatal handi-
cap: "some of the finest narratives in the world—'Gil Blas'
and 'Robinson Crusoe,' for example—have been written
without its employment; and 'The Hutted Knoll,' like
all the sea and forest novels of Cooper, has been made
deeply interesting, although depending upon this peculiar
source of interest not at all. Thus the absence of plot can
never be critically regarded as a *defect;* although its judicious use, in all cases aiding and in no case injuring
other effects, must be regarded as of a very high order of
merit." As a substitute, *Wyandotté* has a three-fold interest: the theme of life in the wilderness (Poe notes sarcas-
tically that only an imbecile author can fail with life in
the forest or on the ocean); the Robinson-Crusoe-like detail of its management; and the portraiture of the half-

civilized Indian, with the setting on the New York frontier at the beginning of the Revolution.[9]

Although he included Catharine M. Sedgwick (in the quite respectable company of Irving, Cooper, Paulding, Bryant, and Halleck) as one whose literary reputation owed much to her being one "of our literary pioneers," Poe thought highly of her novels. In "Autography" he noted that her handwriting "points unequivocally to the traits of her literary style—which are strong common sense, and a masculine disdain of mere ornament." Her best and most popular novels were *Hope Leslie* and *The Linwoods;* these placed her "upon a level with the best of our native novelists. Of American *female* writers we must consider her the first"—a judgment which he qualified in "The Literati," where it is the public rather than Poe that gives her "precedence among our female writers." The prevailing features of *The Linwoods* (which Poe thought the best of her books) were "ease, purity of style, pathos, and verisimilitude. To plot it has little pretension." But he also noted in her work a "very peculiar fault—that of discrepancy between the words and character of the speaker—the fault, indeed, more properly belongs to the depicting of character itself."

Poe felt that several of her feminine contemporaries surpassed her in a single quality, but that in many of the qualities she excelled and in none was particularly deficient. But she was an author of "marked talent" rather than of genius. In attempting to describe the nature of her talent, he makes an interesting comparison: "Miss Sedgwick has now and then been nicknamed 'the Miss Edgeworth of America'; but she has done nothing to bring down upon her the vengeance of so equivocal a title. That she has thoroughly studied and profoundly admired Miss Edgeworth may, indeed, be gleaned from her works—but what woman has not? Of imitation there is not the slightest perceptible taint. In both authors we observe the same tone of thoughtful morality, but here all resemblance ceases. In the Englishwoman there is far more of a certain Scotch prudence, in the American more of warmth, tenderness, sympathy for the weaknesses of her sex. Miss Edgeworth is the more acute, the more inventive and the more rigid. Miss Sedgwick is the more womanly."[10]

Mainly because he honestly admired the novel but in part, perhaps, because he thought the anonymous *George Balcombe* had been written by a close personal friend, Poe in January, 1837, gave it lavish commendation: "George Balcombe thinks, speaks, and acts, as no person, we are convinced, but Judge Beverly Tucker ever precisely thought, spoke, or acted before." Poe gives a lengthy summary of this complex story of a concealed will, and praises especially the trial scene: "Fiction, thus admirably managed, has all the force and essential value of truth." The delineation of characters is excellent, although there is no originality in the characterization: "we mean to say that the merit here is solely that of observation and fidelity. Original characters, so called, can only be critically praised as such, either when presenting qualities known in real life, but never before depicted, (a combination nearly impossible) or when presenting qualities (moral, or physical, or both) which although unknown, or even known to be hypothetical, are so skillfully adapted to the circumstances which surround them, that our sense of fitness is not offended, and we find ourselves seeking a reason why these things *might not have been,* which we are still satisfied *are not.* The latter species of originality appertains to the loftier region of the *Ideal.*"

Here, as elsewhere, Poe make a distinction between style and grammatical correctness. In treating this aspect of *George Balcombe,* he gives one of his clearest state-

ments on the subject: "The general manner is that of a
scholar and gentleman in the best sense of both terms—
bold, vigorous, and rich—abrupt rather than diffuse—and
not over scrupulous in the use of energetic vulgarisms.
With the mere English, some occasional and trivial faults
may be found." As examples, Poe cites the use of technical
terms, of a dangling modifier, and some unclear sentences.
He also noted that the book "bears a strong family resemblance to the Caleb Williams of Godwin." But its
positive merits far outweighed its defects; it held the interest from beginning to end; it had "invention, vigor,
almost audacity of thought"; it had wholeness, with nothing out of place or out of time. As a result, Poe declared
that he was "induced to regard it, upon the whole, as *the
best* American novel."

Poe had been right about the authorship of *George
Balcombe;* he was wrong when he denied that *The Partisan Leader* had been written by Tucker. When he dealt
with Tucker in "Autography," Poe somewhat modified
his earlier judgment: *George Balcombe* was "one of the
best novels . . . although for some reason the book was
never a popular favorite. It was perhaps, somewhat too
didactic for the general taste." He did not mention *The
Partisan Leader,* but noted that he himself had been
thought the author of a highly unfavorable article on the
Pickwick Papers which Tucker had written, whereas Poe
had praised Dickens for a high and just distinction."[11]

It was characteristic of Poe that even in reviewing a
popular novel which he considered worthless, he nevertheless made discerning comments on structure that applied to all novels. Joseph H. Ingraham appealed "always
to the taste of the ultra-romanticists (as a matter, we believe, rather of pecuniary policy than of choice) and thus
is obnoxious to the charge of a certain cut-and-thrust,
blue-fire, melodramaticism." Although he did not be-

lieve that Ingraham "stole" *Lafitte,* he could see little value in this swashbuckling story of the Louisiana pirate except for the historical detail. There were too many items that strained the credulity or dissipated the concentration of the reader. Lafitte fails to recognize and fights with a man whom he has known well. Even worse is the clumsy jumping from one scene to another: "We have, for example, been keeping company with the buccaneers for a few pages—but now they are to make an attack upon some old family mansion. In an instant the buccaneers are dropped for the mansion, and the definite for the indefinite article. In place of *the* robbers proceeding in the course wherein we have been bearing them company, they are suddenly abandoned for *a* house. *A* family mansion is depicted." Somewhat later, the reader is informed that this is the house which the buccaneers were planning to attack. As these quotations indicate, Poe was campaigning against looseness of structure and lack of consistency. At a time when artistry in the novel was not greatly valued, he was advocating a much stricter and more coherent form.[12]

* * *

Poe's commentaries on English novelists were confined almost entirely to writers of his own century. At least in part, this was because as a reviewer he was mainly interested in new books. When he reviewed a reprint of Goldsmith's *Vicar of Wakefield,* he wrote at some length about the illustrations, but of the novel only that it was "one of the most admirable fictions in the language."[13] Poe makes it plain that he thought the tale and the romance to be higher forms of art than the more limited novel. *Robinson Crusoe* seemed to him admirable. Defoe's plotless tale succeeded through "the potent magic of verisimilitude."[14]

At least in the period of the *Messenger* reviews, Poe had no doubt that Scott was the greatest writer of prose fiction in the world. In reviewing Henry F. Chorley's *Conti the Discarded: with other Tales and Fancies* (which he praised as showing a noble, interesting purpose, especially in the attempt to introduce into English literature the type of German art novels that personified individual portions of the Fine Arts), he notes that the title story "bears no little resemblance to that purest, and most enthralling of fictions, the Bride of Lammermuir [*sic*]; and we have once before expressed our opinion of this, the master novel of Scott. It is not too much to say that no modern composition, and perhaps no composition whatever, with the single exception of Cervantes' Destruction of Numantia, approaches so nearly to the proper character of the dramas of Aeschylus, as the magic tale of which Ravenswood is the hero. We are not aware of being sustained by any authority in this opinion—yet we do not believe it the less intrinsically correct."

One opinion, which Poe may have considered earlier, appeared in the same issue. After writing that Bulwer as a novelist was "unsurpassed by any writer living or dead," Poe immediately qualified the judgment: "Scott has excelled him in *many* points, and 'The Bride of Lammermuir' is a better book than any individual work by the author of Pelham—'Ivanhoe' is, perhaps, equal to any."[15]

For the merely popular novelists like G. P. R. James, Harrison Ainsworth, Frederick Marryat, and Charles Lever, Poe had only contempt. They wrote as it were to order, being content with mediocre ideas because these would appeal to the public, and putting in those incidents that would insure popularity. So the ideas of Frederick Marryat were the "common property of the mob; his books crowded incident on incident, without any enriching commentary or philosophy; his characters were frequently stolen from those of Dickens. Its English is slovenly, its events improbable. It was meant for popular consumption, and nothing more."[16]

Occasionally a work of "the highest merit" like Dickens's *Old Curiosity Shop* would seem to rival these works in popularity, but then Poe suddenly remembered that *Harry Lorrequer* and *Charles O'Malley* had surpassed it in "what is properly termed popularity." Excellence may not inevitably make a work unpopular, but these novels by Charles Lever go far toward proving that popularity "is evidence of the book's *demerit*" and that undue popularity indicates that "no extensively *popular* book, in the right application of the term, can be a work of high merit, *as regards those particulars of the work that are popular.*" Dickens succeeded in "uniting all suffrages," but his appeals were different: "It is his close observation and imitation of nature which have rendered him popular, while his higher qualities, with the ingenuity evinced in addressing the general taste, have secured him the good word of the informed and intellectual."[17]

Although he later cooled markedly in his critical estimate, Poe in 1836 had little doubt that Bulwer was the greatest of English writers of fiction. The doubt extended only to the admission that Scott might be his equal, or even his superior. Poe started his review of *Rienzi* by noting that he had "long learned to reverence the fine intellect of Bulwer. We take up any production of his pen with a positive certainty that, in reading it, the wildest passions of our nature, the most profound of our thoughts, the brightest visions of our fancy, and the most ennobling and lofty of our aspirations will, in due turn, be enkindled within us." Yet he was not without worthy rivals. D'Israeli had a more brilliant, lofty, and delicate imagination; Theodore Hook more of wit and "our own" Paulding more of broad humor. Others might equal or surpass him in one particular, but "who is there uniting in one person the imagination, the passion, the humor, the energy, the knowledge of the heart, the artist-like eye, the originality, the fancy, and the learning of Edward Lytton Bulwer."

Rienzi was his best novel—a judgment from which Poe did not deviate in later comments. But it is considerably more than a novel. In sweep and character of composition it is essentially epic rather than dramatic; it is also, in the truest sense, a History. Poe digresses to note that "we shall often discover in Fiction the essential spirit and vitality of Historic Truth—while Truth itself, in many a dull and lumbering archive, shall be found guilty of all the inefficiency of Fiction."

It was vastly superior to *The Last Days of Pompeii* because it was richer, more glowing, more vigorous, but also because it dealt with a period more interesting to us. In a favorable review of Lydia Maria Child's romance of Periclean Athens, *Philothea* (1836), Poe wrote that "We have purely human sympathy in the distantly antique; and this little is greatly weakened by the constant necessity of effort in conceiving *appropriateness* in manners, costume, habits, and modes of thought, so widely at variance with those around us." In *Pompeii*, Bulwer transcended this *genre* through the "stupendousness of its leading event" and the skill with which it was depicted, but his work failed "only in the proportion" that it belonged "to this species."[18]

When in 1841 Poe reviewed *Night and Morning*, with its commonplace yet complex structure, Poe deviated from the book to make one of his most striking and most important definitions:

The word *plot*, as commonly accepted, conveys but an indefinite meaning. Most persons think of it as a simple *complexity;* and into this error even so fine a critic as Augustus William Schlegel has obviously fallen, when he confounds its idea with that of the mere *intrigue* in which the Spanish dramas of Cervantes and Calderon abound. But the greatest involution of incident will not result in plot; which, properly defined, is *that in which no part can be displaced without ruin to the whole.* It may be described as a building so dependently constructed, that to change the position of a single brick is to overthrow the entire fabric. In this definition and description, we of course refer only to that infinite perfection which the true artist bears ever in mind—that unattainable goal to which his eyes are always directed, but of the possibility of attaining which he still endeavours, if wise, to cheat himself into the belief. The reading world, however, is satisfied with a less rigid construction of the term. It is content to think that plot a good one, in which none of the *leading* incidents can be *removed* without *detriment* to the mass.

Poe was not insisting on the necessity of plot. As he had in dealing with Cooper, and using some of the same examples, he emphasized the point that "A good tale may be written without it. Some of the finest fictions in the world have neglected it altogether. We see nothing of it in 'Gil Blas,' in the 'Pilgrim's Progress,' or in 'Robinson Crusoe.' Thus it is not an essential in story-telling at all; although, well managed, within proper limits, it is a thing to be desired. At best it is but a secondary and rigidly artistical merit, for which no merit of a higher class—no merit founded in nature—should be sacrified."

The real misconception was the belief that a true unity could be achieved in a long work:

Very little reflection might have sufficed to convince Mr. Bulwer that narratives, even one-fourth as long as the one now lying upon our table, are *essentially* inadapted to that nice and complex adjustment of incident at which he has made this desperate attempt. In the wire-drawn romances which have been so long fashionable (God only knows how or why) the pleasure we derive (if any) is a composite one, and made up of the respective sums of the various pleasurable sentiments experienced in perusal. Without excessive and fatiguing exertion, inconsistent with legitimate interest, the mind cannot comprehend at one time and in one survey the numerous individual items which go to establish the whole. Thus the high ideal sense of the *unique* is sure to be wanting; for, however absolute in itself be the unity of the novel, it must inevitably fail of appreciation. We speak now of that species of unity which is alone worth the attention of the critic—the unity or totality of *effect*.

Mere length in itself had no artistic value. The talk about continuous and sustained effort seemed to Poe "pure twaddle and nothing more." If a Bulwer insisted on writing long romances simply because they were fashionable, if he could not be satisfied with the brief tale which "admits of the highest development of artistical power in alliance with the wildest vigour of the imagination," then he must content himself with a simple narrative form.[19]

Poe added to his earlier distinction between style and language. The chief constituent of a good style is "what artists have agreed to denominate *tone*." Since Bulwer's tone is always correct, he can scarcely be termed a bad stylist. On the other hand, his English is "turgid, involved, and ungrammatical." Poe cites numerous examples of faulty constructions, and the irritating mannerism of beginning many short sentences with *So*. But Bulwer's predominant failing, in point of style, was "an absolute mania of metaphor—metaphor always running into allegory." Pure allegory was an abomination that appealed only to our faculties of comparison, without interesting our reason or our fancy; metaphor, "its softened image, has indisputable force when sparingly and skillfully employed." Bulwer was neither sparing nor skillful: "He is king-coxcomb of figures of speech."

Poe no longer reverenced Bulwer's intellect, or thought him the first of English novelists. Rather, in a thoughtful summing up, he attempted to assay Bulwer's merits and his place:

> With an intellect rather well balanced than lofty, he has not full claim to the title of a man of genius. Urged by the burning desire of doing much, he has certainly done something. Elaborate even to a fault, he will never write a bad book, and has once or twice been upon the point of concocting a good one. It is the custom to call him a fine writer, but in doing so we should judge him less by an artistical standard of excellence than by comparison with the drivellers who surround him. To Scott he is altogether inferior, except in that mock and tawdry philosophy which the Caledonian had the discretion to avoid, and the courage to condemn. In pathos, humour, and verisimilitude he is unequal to Dickens, surpassing him only in general knowledge and in the sentiment of Art. Of James he is more than the equal at all points. While he could never fall as low as D'Israeli has occasionally fallen, neither himself nor any of those whom we have mentioned have ever risen nearly so high as that very gifted and very extraordinary man.[20]

When he first acclaimed Bulwer, Poe had never heard of Dickens. Four months later (June, 1836) he reviewed *Watkins Tottle, and other Sketches,* by Boz, and claimed that some of them through magazine publication were "old and highly esteemed acquaintances," but of the author he could only say that "we know nothing more than that he is a far more pungent, more witty, and better disciplined writer of sly articles, than nine-tenths of the Magazine writers in Great Britain." These sketches or stories had a great advantage over the usual novel in that each one could be "taken in at one view, by the reader." Poe especially praised "The Black Veil" as an "act of stirring tragedy," and he continued for years to use it as a touchstone of what such a tale should be. His comment on Dickens's method concentrates on the author's absorption in his subject: there are no anecdotes but "we are enveloped in its atmosphere of wretchedness and extortion."

Unfortunately, Poe's mind was still so full of irritation with Colonel William Stone's *Ups and Downs* (which he had "used up" in the same issue) that he employed the sketch for a derogatory comparison: "So perfect, and never-to-be-forgotten a picture cannot be brought about by any such trumpery exertion, or still more trumpery talent, as we find employed in the ineffective daubing of Colonel Stone."[21]

By November, when he reviewed *The Posthumous Papers of the Pickwick Club,* he knew that Boz was Charles Dickens, and the new book, he thought, fully sustained his "high opinion of the comic power and of the rich imaginative conception" of the earlier one. But it was in *The Old Curiosity Shop* that Dickens reached the peak of his genius (Poe was dead before *David Copperfield* and later novels were published). The defects in the story were mainly to be traced to the evils of serial publication. The title itself was a misnomer, for the shop had only a collateral interest, and is spoken of merely in the beginning. Characters are introduced who prove to be supererogatory; incidents that at first seemed necessary turn out to be worthless and are never developed. Yet these were insignificant defects. *The Old Curiosity Shop* embodied "more originality in every point, but in character especially, than any single work within our knowledge." Misguided critics had called some of these persons caricatures, but "the charge is grossly ill-founded. No critical principle is more firmly grounded in reason than that a certain amount of exaggeration is essential in the proper depicting of truth itself. We do not paint an object to be true, but to appear true to the beholder. Were we to copy nature with accuracy, the object copied would seem unnatural." Dicken's characters were not caricatures but creations.

The most noteworthy feature of the book was "its

chaste, vigorous, and glowing *imagination*. This is the one charm, all potent, which alone would suffice to compensate for a world more of error than Mr. Dickens ever committed." The pathos in the concluding scenes "is of that best order which is relieved, in great measure by ideality." The only book that approached it in this respect was Fouqué's *Undine*. But Fouqué was dealing with an imaginary character with purely fanciful attributes, and so "cannot command our full sympathies, as can a simple denizen of earth." These qualities made *The Old Curiosity Shop* "very much the best of the works of Mr. Dickens."

In a carefully reasoned estimate, Poe compared Dickens with Bulwer:

> The Art of Mr. Dickens, although elaborate and great, seems only a happy modification of Nature. In this respect he differs remarkably from the author of "Night and Morning." The latter, by excessive care and patient reflection, aided by much rhetorical knowledge and general information, has arrived at the capability of producing books which might be mistaken by ninety-nine readers out of a hundred for the genuine inspiration of genius. The former, by the promptings of the truest genius itself, has been brought to compose, and evidently without effort, works which have effected a long-sought consummation, which have rendered him the idol of the people, while defying and enchanting the critics. Mr. Bulwer, through art, has almost created a genius. Mr. Dickens, through genius, has perfected a standard from which Art itself will derive its essence, its rules.[22]

Poe may not have been the father of the detective story, but he was certainly the first important critic who attempted to set an aesthetic for the *genre*. Characteristically, this was done in a review of Dickens's *Barnaby Rudge*. He listed explicitly two principles, he suggested a third, and in his practice indicated a fourth.

Under no circumstances may the author in his own

right mislead the reader: no "undue or inartistical means be employed to conceal the secret of the plot." When a character asserted that the body of poor Mr. Rudge was found, this was legitimate and "no misdemeanor against Art in stating what was not the fact; since the falsehood is put into the mouth of Solomon Daisy, and given merely as the impression of this individual and the public. The writer has not asserted it in his own person, but ingeniously conveyed an idea (false in itself, yet a belief in which is necessary for the effect of the tale) by the mouth of one of his characters." On the other hand, it is "disingenuous and inartistical" for the author himself to denominate Mrs. Rudge as "the widow," for the author knows that her husband is not dead.

It is imperative that "the secret be well kept." A failure to preserve the secret until the *denouement* "throws all into confusion, so far as regards the *effect* intended. If the mystery leaks out, against the author's will, his purposes are immediately at odds and ends; for he proceeds upon the supposition that certain impressions *do* exist, which do *not* exist, in the mind of his readers." Poe was uncertain how many readers had solved the mystery in *Barnaby Rudge;* he had done so and had published his analysis immediately after the first installment had appeared. He noted the minor errors that he had made, but correctly insisted that they were minor. For one reader at least, the mystery had not been mysterious enough.

For the story to be legitimately mysterious, the author must to a great extent be engaged in concealing character, whereas the novelist usually was engaged in revealing and developing his characters. This may be done through incidents, such as the occasion when the murderer dresses the corpse of the gardener in his own clothes, puts his ring on its finger and his watch in its pocket—thus deluding the other characters. This may also be done through false or mistaken suspicions, so that an innocent man becomes a prime suspect. Yet this concealment of character should not be done directly by the author, but must be achieved indirectly. It is the purpose of the author to "whet curiosity" in the particulars of the story, as a means of disguising the solution.

These inter-related purposes, as Poe demonstrated in his own stories, can be better achieved through the use of a narrator than by the omniscient author. The narrator does not know everything. He may be duped, or conveniently sent away from the scene so that he had only partial information, or may interpret falsely a key bit of evidence. He must not deliberately present false evidence, but as a character in the story he is absolved from omniscience. This justifies his giving a partial or a mistaken picture, provided he believes that it is a true one.[23]

*   *   *

Poe reviewed only a few foreign novels, and those only in translation. Of these, only one seems to need commentary: the romance *Undine* by the Baron de la Motte Fouqué. This German story of a beautiful but soulless water-spirit who loves and marries a man in order to gain a soul seemed to Poe "what we advisedly consider the finest romance in existence." Poe did not like for a story to have an overt or explicit moral; in *Undine,* the allegorical element was as well-handled as "that most indefensible species of writing" ever could be, for beneath the surface of the story "there runs a mystic or under current of meaning, of the simplest and most easily intelligible, yet of the most richly philosophical character." Its unity was absolute: "every minute point of the picture fills and satisfies the eye. Every thing is attended to, and nothing is out of time or out of place."²⁴

Undine remained for Poe one of the three great prose romances, worthy to be ranked with Scott's *Bride of Lammermoor* and Dickens's *Old Curiosity Shop.* He indicated less enthusiasm for the novel, but he consistently placed *Robinson Crusoe* and *Gil Blas* as the best in that *genre.* It may be worth noting, however, that two of the romances are short enough that they might easily be read at one sitting.

From the beginning of his critical career, Poe was more interested in the short story (which he usually called the tale and sometimes the article) than he was in the novel or romance. In the long work, unity or totality of effect was impossible for the author to achieve, and impossible for the reader to feel or grasp. He wrote repeatedly that the tale offered the greatest challenge to the imagination and the fairest field to the artist of any form of prose fiction. Yet it is also significant that a very early treatment emphasized the relation of the tale to the magazine.

When Thomas W. White, Editor of the *Southern Literary Messenger,* complained that "Berenice" was "far too horrible," Poe admitted that the accusation was justified. But he admitted that only for the individual story, and not for the type:

. . . what I wish to say relates to the character of your Magazine more than to any articles I may offer, and I beg you to believe that I have no intention of giving you *advice,* being fully confident that, upon consideration, you will agree with me. The history of all Magazines shows plainly that those which have attained celebrity were indebted for it to articles *similar in nature—to Berenice*—although, I grant you, far superior in style and execution. I say similar in *nature.* You ask me in what does this nature consist? In the ludicrous heightened into the grotesque: the fearful coloured into the

horrible: the witty exaggerated into the burlesque: the singular wrought out into the strange and mystical. You may say all
this is bad taste. I have my doubts about it. Nobody is more
aware than I am that simplicity is the cant of the day—but
take my word for it no one cares any thing about simplicity
in their hearts. Believe me also, in spite of what people say
to the contrary, that there is nothing easier in the world than
to be extremely simple. But whether the articles of which I
speak are, or are not in bad taste is little to the purpose. To
be appreciated you must be *read,* and these things are invariably sought after with avidity.

In this significant passage, Poe put the emphasis square-
ly on the tale's suitability for a magazine. It must first of
all gain and hold the attention of readers; if it failed to
do that, its virtues were of no practical value.[25]

Poe seems to have thought of Washington Irving as an
essayist and historian rather than as a writer of fiction.
This may have been caused in part by the books which
he reviewed. *The Crayon Miscellany, No. III,* contained
a re-telling of "a few striking and picturesque legends"
of the conquest of Spain by the Saracens; although they
lacked the authenticity of history, they were "partially
facts"; all Irving had done was "to adorn them in his own
magical language." *Astoria* was straightforward history,
executed in "a masterly manner." Only in a side-glance in
a discussion of the skillfully-constructed story does he
grant Irving much merit in this type of writing: "The
'Tales of a Traveller,' by Irving, are graceful and impressive narratives—'The Young Italian' is especially good—
but there is not one of the series which can be commended
as a whole. In many of them the interest is subdivided and
frittered away."

Poe was flattered when Irving praised "The Fall of the
House of Usher" and "William Wilson," although he
seems to have exaggerated somewhat Irving's compliments.
There was a pertinent reason for his delight. Since Irving

"heads the school of the quietists," his approbation would give Poe a "complete triumph over those little critics who would endeavor to put me down by raising the hue & cry of *exaggeration* in style, of *Germanism* and such twaddle."[26]

Although he confessed that he was not generally of a "merry mood," Poe hailed with delight the anonymously-published *Georgia Scenes,* by A. B. Longstreet. He knew nothing of the author, but thought him " a clever fellow, inbued with a spirit of the *truest* humor, and endowed, moreover, with an exquisitely discriminative and penetrating understanding of *character* in general, and of Southern character in particular. And we do not mean to speak of *human* character exclusively. To be sure, our Georgian is *au fait* here too—he is learned in all things appertaining to the biped without feathers. In regard, especially to that class of Southwestern mammalia who come under the generic appellation of 'savagerous wild cats,' he is a very Theophrastus in duodecimo. But he is not the less at home in other matters. Of geese and ganders he is the La Bruyere, and of good-for-nothing horses the Rochefoucault." In spite of this high praise and granting to the author sly humor and an "exquisite dramatic talent," Poe considered the work a collection of sketches rather than of tales; he paraphrased approvingly Longstreet's prefatory statement that "they are, generally, nothing more than fanciful combinations of real incidents and characters," and in some instances literally true. Poe thought the book a landmark in American humor, but not in the development of the American short story.[27]

Except for Hawthorne's work, Poe could in fact find few examples to praise. The British, especially Dickens, were vastly superior. Of skillfully-constructed American tales, perhaps the best was Simms's "Murder Will Out," although it had "some glaring defects." Irving had written graceful and impressive narratives; John Neal's work showed vigor of thought and picturesque combination of incident, but his stories rambled too much and invariably broke down "just before coming to an end." Purely from the point of view of construction (and Poe noted that other points might be more important), the tales of N. P. Willis were consistently the best—"with the exception of Mr. Hawthorne."[28]

Of American story-tellers, only Hawthorne had consistently displayed "an Art subservient to genius of a very lofty order." His distinctive trait was "invention, creation, imagination, originality"—words that Poe here uses as synonyms. True, the originality was a trifle marred by Poe's detecting "something which resembles plagiarism—but which *may be* a very flattering coincidence of thought" in Hawthorne's "Howe's Masquerade." In that story and in his own "William Wilson" the two conceptions are identical, and many points are similar. Poe did not press the accusation, however, but contented himself with suggesting the possibility. Instead, he ended the review on a note of high praise:

> In the way of objection we have scarcely a word to say of these tales. There is, perhaps, a somewhat too general or prevalent *tone*—a tone of melancholy and mysticism. The subjects are insufficiently varied. There is not so much of *versatility* evinced as we might well be warranted in expecting from the high powers of Mr. Hawthorne. But beyond these trivial exceptions we have really none to make. The style is purity itself. Force abounds. High imagination gleams from every page. Mr. Hawthorne is a man of the truest genius. We only regret that the limits of our Magazine will not permit us to pay him that full tribute of commendation, which, under other circumstances, we should be so eager to pay.[29]

In 1847, Poe sharply although somewhat confusedly revised his earlier opinion as to Hawthorne's originality. He treated "all subjects in a similar tone of dreamy *in-*

nuendo, yet in this walk he evinces extraordinary genius."
But his treatment of subject-matter was too monotonously
alike for him to be called truly original: "This true or
commendable originality, however, implies not the uni-
form, but the continuous peculiarity—a peculiarity springing from ever-active vigor of fancy—better still if from
ever-present force of imagination, giving its own hue, its
own character to everything it touches, and, especially,
self-impelled to touch everything." By this stringent definition, Hawthorne was not really original; moreover, he
owed too much to the manner of the German Tieck.
There was a "sameness, or monotone" in Hawthorne's
work; this was the "strain of allegory which completely
overwhelms the greater number of his subjects, and which
in some measure interferes with the direct conduct of
absolutely all." Since Poe felt that in defence of allegory
"there is scarcely one respectable word to be said," it is
hardly surprising that he qualified his praise of Hawthorne. Even so, he makes a useful aesthetic point: "if
allegory ever establishes a fact, it is by dint of overturning
a fiction. Where the suggested meaning runs through the
obvious one in a *very* profound under-current so as never
to interfere with the upper one without our own volition,
so as never to show itself unless *called* to the surface, there
only, for the proper uses of fictitious narrative, is it available at all. Under the best circumstances, it must always
interfere with that unity of effect which to the artist, is
worth all the allegory in the world."

Poe's dislike of the Transcendentalists may in part have
motivated these strictures. He was willing to allow many
virtues to the literary artist, but Hawthorne's "spirit of
'metaphor run-mad' is clearly imbibed from the phalanx
and phalanstery atmosphere in which he has been so long
struggling for breath. He has not half the material for
the exclusiveness of authorship that he possesses for its

universality. He has the purest style, the finest taste, the most available scholarship, the most delicate humor, the most touching pathos, the most radiant imagination, the most consummate ingenuity; and with these varied good qualities he has done *well* as a mystic. But is there any one of these qualities which would prevent his doing doubly as well in a career of honest, upright, sensible, prehensible and comprehensible things? Let him mend his pen, get a bottle of visible ink, come out from the Old Manse, cut Mr. Alcott, hang (if possible) the editor of 'The Dial,' and throw out of the window to the pigs all his odd numbers of 'The North American Review'."[30]

When one considers that Hawthorne was his only serious or worthy rival in the writing of tales, Poe's criticism in 1842 seems not only just but amazingly generous. There are a few quibbles, beginning with the title, *Twice-Told Tales*. They were really thrice-told, and many of them were properly essays rather than tales. In themselves the essays were excellent, their predominant feature being "*repose*. There is no attempt at effect. All is quiet, thoughtful, subdued. Yet this repose may exist simultaneously with high originality of thought; and Mr. Hawthorne has demonstrated the fact. At every turn we meet with novel combinations; yet these combinations never surpass the limits of the quiet.... The Essays of Hawthorne have much of the character of Irving, with more of originality, and less of finish; while, compared with the Spectator, they have a vast superiority at all points."

Yet they were inferior to the tales in polish and interest. It was characteristic of Poe that before reviewing the stories he digressed far enough to give his own idea of what a tale should be. He had no doubt that it afforded "unquestionably the fairest field for the exercise of the loftiest talent, which can be afforded by the domains of mere prose." The best display of literary genius was in

the rhymed poem that was long enough to produce an
intense and enduring impression but brief enough to be
read at one sitting, in not more than an hour. Second only
to this was "the short prose narrative, requiring from a
half-hour to one or two hours in its perusal." The ordinary novel was objectionable because of its length, which
deprived it of "the immense force derivable from *totality.*" Since the tale could be read at one sitting and without distraction, the "soul of the reader is at the writer's
control." This had its disadvantages. The novelist could
wander and digress; he could stop one line of action to
"bring up" another one; he could move freely from character to character and from incident to incident. Since
unity of effect was impossible, he did not have to be so
much concerned with it. But these advantages were gained
at the expense of artistry and of totality; they were in fact
when considered properly not advantages at all. Genius
would not make such sacrifices to expediency.[31]

Poe was the first critic to consider the short story seriously as a literary type and as an independent art form.
Unhesitatingly and often, he declared it to be superior to
the novel. He wanted to define what it was and what it
should be. He desired to develop an aesthetic for a *genre*
that, although by no means new, had been unfairly and
uncomprehendingly deprecated. It was second only to the
lyric poem as a work of art.

This may have been rationalization, as Joseph Wood
Krutch and other writers have baldly declared: Poe may
have been justifying his own inability to write a sustained
work, in prose or verse. It seems more likely that he was,
consciously or unconsciously, setting an aesthetic for an
appropriate magazine fiction. The story must gain and
hold attention in competition with poems, essays, articles,
and reviews. It must for this purpose have a complete and
rounded plot, yet it must be short enough to be published

in one issue. So in 1842 he defined clearly his own ideal of what a story should be, and in 1847 he retained the basic ideas with only slight changes in wording:

A skilful literary artist has constructed a tale. If wise, he has not fashioned his thoughts to accommodate his incidents; but having conceived, with deliberate care, a certain unique or single *effect* to be wrought out, he then invents such incidents—he then combines such events as may best aid him in establishing this preconceived effect. If his very initial sentence tend not to the outbringing of this effect, then he has failed in his first step. In the whole composition there should be no word written, of which the tendency, direct or indirect, is not to the one pre-established design. And by such means, with such care and skill, a picture is at length painted which leaves in the mind of him who contemplates it with a kindred art, a sense of the fullest satisfaction. The idea of the tale has been presented unblemished, because undisturbed; and this is an end unattainable by the novel. Undue brevity is just as exceptionable here as in the poem; but undue length is yet more to be avoided.[32]

Here, clearly stated, is Poe's ideal of prose fiction. It does not sound like rationalization; it has the authentic ring, rather, of a carefully-developed theory that had been evolved not only out of Poe's own practice but as an inevitable result of his critical precepts. The critic reviewing Bulwer's *Night and Morning* was not concerned with his own fiction but with the inadequacy of the novel as an art-form; the critic who so generously praised Hawthorne's stories did not need to call attention to his own work. He desired unity or totality of effect, both in the work itself and on the reader. In fiction, this could only be achieved through the tale. He desired also to edit a good, even a great, magazine, and he thought continually about a literature suited for this purpose. It was not by accident that his theory of fiction set an aesthetic for a magazine literature.

LECTURE
THREE

Poe on Poetry

IN THE PREFATORY LETTER TO THE 1831 POEMS, EDGAR
Allen Poe indicated several lines of critical thought that
he was to refine and develop in later reviews and articles.
These remarks are limited to his commentary on poetry.
There are no less than five of these: his belief that very
few readers liked epics, whatever they might say to the
contrary, with the casual aside that Milton no doubt preferred *Comus* to *Paradise Lost* or *Paradise Regained*—"if
so—justly"; the second, a denial that the metaphysical
ideas of the Lake School of English Poets were a proper
subject-matter for poetry, and a vigorous attack on didacticism, especially as exemplified in the work of Wordsworth; the other three concepts (pleasure, indefiniteness,
musicality) he combined into one paragraph that, unfortunately in the first clause, draws too closely on Coleridge
for comfort: "A poem, in my opinion, is opposed to a
work of science by having, for its *immediate* object, pleasure, not truth; to romance, by having for its object an

indefinite instead of a *definite* pleasure, being a poem only so far as this object is attained; romance presenting perceptible images with definite, poetry with *in*definite sensations, to which end music is an *essential,* since the comprehension of sweet sound is our most indefinite conception. Music, when combined with a pleasurable idea, is poetry; music without the idea is simply music; the idea without the music is prose from its very definitiveness."[1]

Two years earlier, in "Sonnet—To Science," Poe had complained that factual knowledge had destroyed the romance and the mystery of life, that for the poet the rational mind was less satisfying than intuition. He extended this idea in the Letter when he declared that "learning has little to do with the imagination—intellect with the passions—or age with poetry." This throws almost all the emphasis on the imagination, and almost none on the intellect or reason.

These ideas mark the beginning, however rudimentary, of Poe's later definitions of poetry. Only the concept of the function of imagination and reason was to be radically changed. To his own satisfaction at least, he had swept out of the domain of poetry all philosophical and didactic verse; he had given a tentative broom-push against long poems. In the end, his experience as a magazine poet and editor, and his theories about pleasure, indefiniteness, and musicality, led him to argue that epic, narrative, and dramatic works were not true poems, even if they were written in verse. Only the subjective lyric deserved the name of a legitimate poem.

He arrived at this conclusion slowly. The most famous of contemporary American poets, William Cullen Bryant, posed something of a problem. In 1840, his poetic reputation was higher at home and abroad "than that of any other American." He had great abilities and positive excellence, but the public was wrong in thinking "Thanatopsis" his greatest poem. He had the negative merit of almost faultless versification; his utterances were often noble and sometimes moving. But it was as a literary pioneer (along with Irving, Paulding, and Cooper) that he deserved greatest honor. His defect was that "the objects in the moral or physical universe coming within the periphery of his vision" were too limited; for this reason, Poe ranked him below the "spiritual Shelleys," or Coleridges, or Wordsworths, or Keats, or even Tennysons, for the "relative extent of these peripheries of poetical vision must ever be a primary consideration in our classification of poets."[2]

It is not in his rather cursory treatments of Bryant but in his long, thoughtful review of the *Poems* of Joseph Rodman Drake and Fitz-Greene Halleck in April, 1836, that Poe revealed a notable development in his poetic theory. After demanding that American books be judged by international critical standards and remarking that he would make no generalities which were not founded on an analysis of the work itself, Poe made the first of many distinctions between the sentiment of poesy, and the actual poem. The feeling arises from the instinct given to man by God; it is close kin to "the Faculty of Ideality—which is the sentiment of Poesy. This sentiment is the sense of the beautiful, of the sublime, and of the mystical. . . . Poesy is the sentiment of Intellectual Happiness here, and the Hope of a higher Intellectual Happiness hereafter.

"Imagination is its soul. With the *passions* of mankind—although it may modify them greatly—although it may exalt, or inflame, or purify, or control them—it would require little ingenuity to prove that it has no inevitable, and indeed no necessary co-existence." Yet the power of man is strictly limited: "Imagination is, possibly, in man, a lesser degree of the creative power of God. What the

Deity imagines, *is,* but *was not* before. What man imagines *is,* but *was* also. The mind of man cannot imagine what *is not."*

A poem is the practical result, expressed in words, of this poetic sentiment in certain individuals. This sentiment, he noted later, might be expressed in music, painting, sculpture, landscape architecture; or it might remain a subjective and internal emotion. When it took the form of a poem, the genesis of the work was in the imagination. But that in itself was no longer enough. In giving objective form to the feeling, a high degree of artistry was required.

Here Poe made one of his sharpest breaks with the general line of Romantic criticism. A poem was not, and should not be, a means of self-expression. We should judge a poem not by what the writer has felt, but by how successfully he has succeeded in communicating that sentiment: "a poem is not the Poetic faculty, but the *means* of exciting it in mankind." The unaided Ideality could attain this only by accident, whereas a careful artist might, without "being himself imbued with the Poetic Sentiment," nonetheless write a fine poem and succeed in arousing Ideality in his readers. Halleck and Drake had partially succeeded; the man who "of all writers, living or dead," has aroused "most purely, most exclusively, and most powerfully the imaginative faculties in men—owed his extraordinary and almost magical pre-eminence rather to metaphysical than poetical powers. We allude to the author of Christabel, of the Rime of the Ancient Mariner, and of Love—to Coleridge."[3]

After noting that in 1836 no American poets (except perhaps for Bryant) were held in higher esteem than Drake and Halleck, Poe embarked on an exhaustive analysis of Drake's "Culprit Fay." Assuredly he attempts to be fair with his readers. He gives lengthy quotations from this

poem about the love of a fairy for a mortal, and he ex-
amines individual words and phrases for meaning and
for melodic suggestibility. There were a few excellent
passages; Drake sometimes revealed ideality, although not
of a high order. If some passages evinced a degree of imagination, the complete poem did not, in plot, conception,
or general execution. The author had, instead, "a very
moderate endowment of the faculty of Comparison—which
is the chief constituent of *Fancy* or the powers of combination. A thousand such lines may be composed without ex-
ercising in the least degree the Poetic Sentiment, which is
Ideality, Imagination, or the creative ability."

Although widely praised, Halleck's poems were inferior
to Drake's. The prevailing feature of Halleck's muse was
a "quiet air of grace, both in thought and expression," but
even in a serious poem he would try to combine "the low
burlesque with the ideal." Near the end of "Alnwick
Castle" he was guilty of writing "Men in the coal and
cattle line." This might lay claim to oddity, but nothing
more, and it destroyed the unity of effect of a poem that
had started in a delicate manner. In "Marco Bozzaris,"
Halleck had attempted to substitute force for ideal beauty,
depending entirely on "a well ordered and sonorous arrangement of the metre, and a judicious disposal of the
circumstances of the poem" to bring out to the greatest
advantage the death of the Greek patriot in his struggles
against the Turks. The elegy was appealing because of its
subject-matter, but Poe preferred "the union of tender sentiment and simplicity" that he found in the elegy on Drake.

Here, too, Poe showed indications of the obsession
about originality that was to do even greater harm to his
critical reputation than his weakness for personal ridicule.
Halleck's quatrain beginning "Green be the turf above
thee" bore, he thought, "too close a resemblance to the
still more beautiful lines of William Wordsworth, 'She

dwelt among the untrodden ways'." Certainly there is no startling originality in either quatrain, for the ideas in each had been expressed centuries earlier, but the stanzas have no specific relation to each other. Only a mind desperately hunting for plagiarism could have found it in Halleck's verse.[4]

In his reviewing, Poe was notoriously kind to lady poets. In part this can be traced to his chivalrous attitude toward women; in part, also, because he felt that this pleasant but definitely minor work did not merit a critical attack. One exception was Lydia Sigourney. Her compositions were creditable enough, but in acquiring the title of "the American Mrs. Hemans" she stood "palpably convicted of that sin which in poetry is not to be forgiven." The very phrase, Poe thought, spoke loudly in accusation but it was deserved: both in the character of her subjects and in the structure of her versification and even in certain mannerisms, Mrs. Sigourney was an imitator. Perhaps the worst fault of both was that neither woman trusted a poem to be complete within itself. Too often, initial mottoes or quotations or historic facts were prefixed, to explain the meaning of the poem. In a work of magnitude, the reader "is pleased—if at all—with particular passages," but in shorter poems like those of Mrs. Sigourney the effect "will depend, in a very great degree, upon the perfection of its finish, upon the nice adaptation of its constituent parts, and especially upon what is rightly termed by Schlegel, 'the *unity or totality of interest*'." When the meaning of a work of art depends on facts outside of the work itself, "the *totality* of effect is annihilated." For the same reason, he objected to Elizabeth Oakes Smith's using introductory prose arguments, after the manner of Milton, for the sound aesthetic reason that "Every work of art should contain within itself all that is required for its comprehension."

But critics have been too willing to see literary log-rolling in what seems quite honest criticism. Poe's criticism of Thomas Holley Chivers, that he was "at the same time one of the best and one of the worst poets in America," remains a sound judgment, and his poems have, as Poe noted, the "air of a rapt soliloquy." Although he was by no means as original as Poe thought him, Chivers was indeed capable of "snatches of sweet unsustained song. Even his worst nonsense (and some of it is horrible) has an indefinite charm of sentiment and melody. . . . Yet there are as fine individual passages to be found in the poems of Dr. Chivers as in those of any poet whatsoever."[5]

Poe was, although somewhat gropingly, working his way toward a rounded concept of beauty. This concept of totality of effect is of central importance in Poe's criticism and poetry, since he believed that beauty should be the sole province of the poem, but he had to reconcile two apparently contradictory ideas of beauty. He believed that Francis Bacon was correct when he wrote that there is "no exquisite beauty without some strangeness in the proportions." In literature, strangeness or, more specifically, novelty arouses "profound interest in the heart or intellect of man." Yet beauty also meant harmony, order, proportion. In music and in versification, equality seemed to be *"the root of all beauty."*[6]

In part, the emphasis on strangeness and novelty may be traceable to his new (and temporary) conception of the functions of imagination and of fancy. He could no longer believe with Coleridge that the fancy combines, the imagination creates. This was a distinction without a difference, even in degree. The fancy as nearly creates as the imagination; and neither creates in any respect. All novel conceptions are merely unusual combinations. The mind of man can imagine nothing which has not really existed. The distinction that Poe sought to make was that the im-

agination provided those qualities of mind which lifted a
work into the realm of the ideal. It is closely related to the
term *mystic,* as employed by A. W. Schlegel, to denominate "that class of composition in which there lies beneath
the transparent upper current of meaning an under or
suggestive one. What we vaguely term the *moral* of any
sentiment is its mystic or secondary expression. It has the
vast force of an accompaniment of music. This vivifies the
air; that spiritualizes the *fanciful* conception, and lifts it
into the *ideal.*"[7]

Yet Poe was not prepared to abate in any particular his
demand for originality. If this could be achieved only
through the unexpected combinations of novel, strange
or even well-known incidents, it was still worth striving
for. Poetry was a response to a natural, irrepressible, yet
two-fold demand: "Its first element is the thirst for supernal beauty—a beauty which is not afforded the soul by
any existing collocation of earth's forms—a beauty which,
perhaps, *no possible* combination of these forms would
fully produce. Its second element is the attempt to satisfy
this thirst by *novel* combinations, *of those combinations
which our predecessors, toiling in chase of the same phan-
tom, have already set in order.* We thus clearly deduce the
novelty, the *originality,* the *invention,* the *imagination,* or
lastly the *creation* of BEAUTY (for the terms as here employed are synonymous) as the essence of all Poesy." But
the parts must be welded into a unified whole, and this
could best be done through "the combining or binding
force." Only through the strictest proportion and adaptation of all the poetical requisites, only through the se-
verest fitting of each part into its proper place, could a
true harmony and unity be attained.

In his review of Longfellow's *Ballads and Other Poems*
(1842), Poe found fault with "the too obtrusive nature of
their didacticism," and with the author's willingness to

sacrifice invention and imagery for the sake of inculcating a moral. This did not imply a disrespect for the truth, but a limitation on its modes of inculcation:

To convey "the true" we are required to dismiss from the attention all inessentials. We must be perspicuous, precise, terse. We need concentration rather than expansion of mind. We must be calm, unimpassioned, unexcited—in a word, we must be in that peculiar mood which, as nearly as possible, is the exact converse of the poetical. He must be blind indeed who cannot perceive the radical and chasmal difference between the truthful and the poetical modes of inculcation. He must be grossly wedded to conventionalisms, who, in spite of this difference, shall still attempt to reconcile the obstinate oils and waters of Poetry and Truth.

Dividing the world of mind into its most obvious and immediately recognisable distinctions, we have the pure intellect, taste, and the moral sense. We place *taste* between the intellect and the moral sense, because it is just this intermediate space which, in the mind, it occupies. It is the connecting link in the triple chain.

It serves to sustain a mutual intelligence between the extremes. It appertains, in strict appreciation, to the former, but is distinguished from the latter by so faint a difference, that Aristotle has not hesitated to class some of its operations among the Virtues themselves. But the *offices* of the trio are broadly marked. Just as conscience, or the moral sense, recognises duty; just as the intellect deals with *truth;* so is it the part of taste alone to inform us of BEAUTY. And Poesy is the handmaiden but of Taste. Yet we would not be misunderstood. This handmaiden is not forbidden to moralise—in her own fashion. She is not forbidden to depict—but to reason and preach, of virtue. As, of this latter, conscience recognises the obligation, so intellect teaches the expediency, while taste contents herself with displaying the beauty: waging war with vice merely on the ground of its inconsistency with fitness, harmony, proportion.

In a recapitulation, Poe defined the "Poetry of words as the *Rhythmical Creation of Beauty*. Beyond the limits of Beauty its province does not extend. Its sole arbiter is taste. With the intellect or with the Conscience it has only collateral relations. It has no dependence, except incidentally, upon either Duty or *Truth*." With this definition in mind Poe ruled out of the domain of poetry the philosophical works exemplified by Pope's "Essay on Man," which might well be content with the title of an "Essay in Rhyme," and satirically humorous ones such as Butler's "Hudibras." These particular works had great and peculiar merits, but they were not the merits of poetry.[8]

If didacticism, philosophy, metaphysics, satire, and humor were improper subjects for poetry, the inclusion of an ethical or a moral content was not only permissible but desirable. Here the all-important question was the manner of handling. This is perhaps more exactly stated in his comments on James Russell Lowell's "Legend of Brittany" (which he thought "decidedly the noblest poem, of the same length, written by an American") than in the quotation given above: "After every few words of narration, comes a page of morality. Not the morality, *here*—not that the reflections deduced from the incidents, are peculiarly exceptionable, but that they are too obviously, intrusively, and artificially introduced." The moral content should be woven into the texture of the work; it should be suggested rather than stated, as it was in the *Old Curiosity Shop* and in *Undine;* it should be implicit rather than explicit.[9] Near the end of "The Philosophy of Composition," he indicated his own usage in "The Raven": he added an under-current of meaning to the last two stanzas, and their suggestiveness was made "to pervade all the narrative" which had preceded them. As Poe explained, it is this under-current which "imparts to a work of art so much of the *richness* . . . which we are too fond of confounding with *the ideal*. It is the *excess* of the suggested meaning— it is the rendering this the upper instead of the under current of the theme" which turns poetry into prose. By this legitimate use of an indefinite meaning, he attempted to make the raven "emblematical of *Mournful and Never-Ending Remembrance.*" But the good artist would never state this directly to the reader; he leaves it to be inferred. In more modern terms, the entire poem should be the communication.[10]

* * *

The positive evidence that Poe believed only lyric poems to be true poetry is so voluminous that I have been able to give only a relatively few examples. Although less voluminous, the negative evidence is by no means negligible. He stated repeatedly that, in fiction or in poetry, length or extent or bulk was no sign of excellence. The sustained effort that brought forth a three-decker novel or an epic might be a reason to commend the author for the effort (although even of this Poe was doubtful), but it was no reason for praising the work on the effort's account: "It is to be hoped that common sense, in the time to come, will prefer deciding upon a work of art, rather by the impression it makes, by the effect it produces, than by the time it took to impress the effect or by the amount of 'sustained effort' which had been found necessary in effecting the impression. The fact is, that perseverance is one thing, and genius quite another."

He was prepared to maintain that the phrase "a long poem" was "simply a flat contradiction in terms." He based this statement on his doctrine of unity of effect; on his experience as a magazine editor and poet; and above all on his belief that elevating excitement of the soul was by a "psychal necessity" transient. He found evidence of this in several highly-praised epics. The *Iliad*, he believed, was originally intended as a series of lyrics; if not, it was an artistic anomaly. A prejudiced child of his own age, Poe thought that Richard H. Horne's *Orion* was "one of the noblest epics in any language" and for it he showed an uncritical and almost unrestrained enthusiasm, but he noted that he reserved this enthusiasm for certain passages and pictures.

His definitive statement on the epic, hinted at in the 1831 prefatory Letter, goes back to a poet whom he admired but did not especially like, John Milton:

> There are, no doubt, many who have found difficulty in reconciling the critical dictum that the "Paradise Lost" is to be devoutly admired throughout, with the absolute impossibility of maintaining for it, during perusal, the amount of enthusiasm which that critical dictum would demand. This great work, in fact, is to be regarded as poetical, only when, losing sight of that vital requisite in all works of Art, Unity, we view it merely as a series of minor poems. If, to preserve its Unity—its totality of effect or impression—we read it (as would be necessary) at a single sitting, the result is but a constant alternation of excitement and depression. After a passage of what we feel to be true poetry, there follows, inevitably, a passage of platitude which no critical pre-judgment can force us to admire; but if, upon completing the work, we read it again; omitting the first book—that is to say, commencing with the second—we shall be surprised at now finding that admirable which we before condemned—that damnable which we had previously so much admired. It follows from all this that the ultimate, aggregate, or absolute effect of even the best epic under the sun, is a nullity:—and this is precisely the fact.[11]

Yet it was not the concept of the epic in itself which was at fault. The error was in the concept of poetry, and with that a confusion of *genres*. Although he preferred *Comus* to Milton's other works and his own nearly completed play, *Politian*, was in verse, he was convinced that there should be no such genus as a closet drama. In Longfellow's *Spanish Student* there were some beautiful passages, but "it is only when we separate the poem from the drama, that it can be said to have merit of any kind. For, in fact, it is only when we separate the poem from the drama, that the passages we have commended as beautiful can be understood to have beauty. We are not too sure, indeed, that a 'dramatic poem' is not a flat contradiction in terms. At all events a man of true genius, (and such Mr. L. unquestionably is,) has no business with these hybrid and paradoxical compositions. Let a poem be a poem only; let a play be a play and nothing more." This uncompromising judgment may explain why Poe never finished *Politian* or made any effort to get it considered for production. He had no doubt that the two forms had different purposes: "The object of poetry in general, is beauty—the object of the drama, which has nothing to do with poetry, unless through the introduction of a poetical *character,* is the *portraiture of nature in human action and earthly incident.*"[12] The dramatist should surpass nature in combining events with character, so as to give a heightened impression upon the audience, but the stage could not be filled with puppets or with unrealistic characters. Reviewing Anna Cora Mowatt's *Fashion,* he declared that there was "not one particle of any nature beyond greenroom nature, about it. No such events ever happened in fact, or ever could happen, as happen in 'Fashion'. . . . Our fault-finding is on the score of deficiency in verisimilitude—in natural art—that is to say, in art based in the natural laws of man's heart and understanding." The drama was to help man to understand himself on earth; poetry was to lift him in mind and spirit above the earth.[13]

His belief that the play should be a representation of human actions led him to the conclusion that a "closet-drama is an anomaly—a paradox—a mere figure of speech. There should be no such things as closet-dramas. The proof of the dramatism is the capacity for representation."[14] Although he derived great pleasure from attending performances, and read and reviewed many plays, he showed little enthusiasm for the drama as an art-form. It was the most imitative of all the arts. He rated Aeschylus's *Prometheus Vinctus* as one of the supreme literary creations, but "Euripides and Sophocles were merely echoes of Aeschylus, and not only was Terence Menander and nothing beyond, but of the sole Roman tragedies extant, (the ten attributed to Seneca,) nine are on Greek subjects." After seeing *Antigone* performed, he concluded that there was about it as well as "about all the ancient plays, an insufferable baldness, or platitude, the inevitable result of inexperience in Art—but a baldness, nevertheless, which pedantry would force us to believe the result of a studied and supremely artistic simplicity alone." Yet in spite of these doubts, Poe quoted from or referred to Aeschylus thirteen times, Sophocles seven, Euripides six. His critical comments were not based on unfamiliarity.[15]

The Greek drama he undoubtedly read in translation; that of Shakspeare and the Elizabethans he knew at first-hand, and so well that, for one example, he quoted from *Hamlet* thirty-eight times. He had two qualifications. The first was not applicable to the plays themselves. Poe objected to the type of Shakspeare hero-worshippers, encouraged by Carlyle, who "rant about him, lecture about him— about *him, him,* and nothing else—for no other reason than that he is utterly beyond their comprehension." This did not imply a lack of recognition of greatness; rather, the proper attitude for gifted individuals was to "kneel around the summit, beholding, face to face, the master spirit who stands upon the pinnacle." The second qualification had to do more with his own time than with the Elizabethan. The modern drama was entirely too imitative, and it had retained too many unnatural and outworn stage conventions, such as the soliloquy and the aside.

Dramatists must learn to apply *"principles* of dramatic composition" that were "founded in Nature, and in common sense."

Almost always, Shakspeare had done this, although Poe thought the whole design of *The Taming of the Shrew* "not only unnatural but an arrant impossibility. The heart of no woman could ever have been reached by brute violence." But the original had much of nature and truth in it; the modern adaptation by Colley Cibber was "absolutely beneath contempt." The great plays suffered only from being misunderstood and misinterpreted. Men treat the characters not as "the coinage of a human brain, but as if they had been actual existences on earth. We talk of Hamlet the man, instead of Hamlet the *dramatis personae* —of Hamlet that God, in place of Hamlet that Shakspeare created." The dramatist had deliberately yet with artistic justification exaggerated the insanity of the Dane. He felt that this was his right, "felt it through his marvellous power of *identification* with humanity at large—the ultimate source of his magical influence upon mankind."[16]

The modern drama was alive, but it was moribund. A few good plays had been written in the United States; among them, N. P. Willis's *Tortesa the Usurer,* in spite of its being cluttered with incidental intrigue and being a "mere succession of incidents," and Robert Conrad's *Aylmere,* especially in the development of the main character, Jack Cade. There were innumerable bad plays, including the tremendously popular *London Assurance* by Dion Boucicault, which seemed to Poe "the most inane and utterly despicable of all modern comedies." The best of living dramatists was Bulwer-Lytton, his best play *The Lady of Lyons:* "It abounds in sentiments which stir the soul as the sound of a trumpet. It proceeds rapidly and consequentially; the interest not for one minute being allowed to flag. Its incidents are admirably conceived and skillfully wrought into execution. Its *dramatis personae,* throughout, have the high merit of being natural, although, except in the case of Pauline, there is no marked individuality. She is a creation which would have done no dishonor to Shakspeare." All in all, Poe thought Bulwer better as a dramatist than as a novelist.[17]

Poe revealed even less enthusiasm for the long narrative poem than he did for the epic. In his own time, the best of such poets was Thomas Moore (Anacreon Moore, Poe called him), with *Lalla Rookh* and, even better, with *Alciphron.* Moore was unrivalled in general dexterity and in melody of versification; he rarely reached the heights of poetry, but his radiance had an equable glow and he possessed a "vivid fancy, an epigrammatic spirit, a fine taste," and no little degree of imagination. Yet the success of *Alciphron* depended to a surprising degree on a non-poetical element: "to the facility with which he recounts a poetical story in a *prosaic* way. By this is meant that he preserves the tone and method of arrangement of prose relation, and thus obtains great advantages over his more stilted compeers. His is no poetical *style* (such, for example, as the French have—a distinct style for a distinct purpose,) but an easy and ordinary prose manner, *ornamented into poetry.*" This is certainly qualified praise; it also explains why Poe had small liking for narrative poems.[18]

Poe's obsession about plagiarism led him into the least fortunate of his literary battles. His attack on the New York *Knickerbocker* clique and its arrogant puffing of the books of the group had earned him powerful enemies, but it had brought to his side powerful supporters; his virulent attacks on Longfellow alienated most of his friends and admirers. It should be noted here that as long as Poe confined his accusations to those of imitativeness,

he again had numerous and powerful allies. The two
attacks were not unconnected. Lewis Gaylord Clark and
his coterie had adopted Longfellow as the distinctive, unsurpassed American poet who could do no poetic wrong.
Undoubtedly this undiscriminating puffery by his enemies
infuriated Poe; it helps to explain, although it does not
justify, Poe's accusations. But it is another good example
of Poe's approach to literature from the point of view of
a magazine editor.

When Poe reviewed *Voices of the Night* (1840), he
remarked that when he had first read "Hymn to the
Night" he was convinced that "a poet of high genius had
at length arisen amongst us." The book rather shook his
faith in that preliminary judgment: it revealed that Longfellow had something of genius and imagination and "the
loftiest qualities of the poetical soul," but he lacked the
combining force and therefore had 'nothing of unity" even
in the best of the poems. Poe may have been a bit captious
in pointing out defects in the poems, but at least he indicated clearly the reasons for his objections.

There seems less reason for his charging Longfellow, in
his "Midnight Mass for the Dying Year," with having
copied Tennyson's "Death of the Old Year." But Poe's
rationalizations are important in that they give some idea
of his peculiar ideas, for this was a plagiarism "too palpable to be mistaken, and which belongs to the most barbarous class of literary robbery: that class in which, while
the words of the wronged author are avoided, his most in-
tangible, and therefore his least defensible and least re-
claimable property is purloined." Then, oddly since the
concept goes back in folklore at least to very early re-
corded literature, Poe added that nearly all of value in
Tennyson's poem is the "conception of personifying the
Old Year as a dying old man, with the singularly wild and
fantastic *manner* in which that conception is carried out.

Of this conception and of this manner he is robbed." To-day there seems nothing remarkable in originality, in manner, or in literary value in either poem, but the charge of plagiarism is at best dubious. Both men were drawing on a well-known conventional personification, and both wrote good but conventional poems on the subject.

Longfellow contented himself with a denial, but Clark unwisely stated that it was Tennyson who had stolen from Longfellow, or at the most that Poe had charged only an imitation of Tennyson. Poe accepted the challenge. He did not say that "Professor Longfellow's poem is 'imitated' from Tennyson. He calls it a bare-faced and barbarous plagiarism." In his own defense, Poe added that he had reprinted both poems, so that readers could judge for themselves the justice of his accusation.[19]

Poe did not allow these beliefs to blind him as to Longfellow's merits as a poet, or to his value as a magazine contributor, to his own projected *Penn Magazine,* and to *Graham's.* Poe's magazine remained in the land of dreams, but Longfellow soon became one of the prized contributor's to *Graham's.* This betrays an ambivalence on Poe's part toward Longfellow's work that is characteristic yet logical: he liked many of Longfellow's poems and, until Lowell's work appeared, rated him as the best of American poets, but if he was "entitled to the first place among the poets of America," it must at the same time be said that he was guilty of "an imitation sometimes verging upon downright theft."

The crux, however, came in Poe's accusation that Longfellow had stolen directly from Poe's own work. Somewhat earlier, Poe had praised highly "The Beleaguered City"; somehow, he had come to believe that Longfellow's poem was merely a re-writing of his own "Haunted Palace": "I first published the H. P. in Brooks' 'Museum,' a monthly journal of Baltimore, now dead. Afterward, I embodied it in a tale called 'The House of Usher,' in Burton's Magazine. Here it was, I suppose, that Prof. Longfellow saw it; for, about six weeks afterwards, there appeared in the South. Lit. Mess.: a poem by him called 'The Beleaguered City,' which may now be found in his volume *Voices of the Night.* The identity in title is striking; for by the Haunted Palace I mean to imply a mind haunted by phantoms—a disordered brain—and by the Beleaguered City Prof. L. means just the same. But the tournoure of the poem is based upon mine." Poe's chronology is correct and to some of us "The Haunted Palace" is his finest poem, but the idea behind it does not seem so unique that another poet could not have arrived at it independently. Poe was never willing to allow for the long arm of coincidence.[20]

Poe was infuriated by an article in the English magazine, the *Foreign Quarterly Review,* which acclaimed Longfellow as "unquestionably the first" of American poets (a statement with which Poe agreed) and the only original poet in the United States because his "mind was educated in Europe" (the anonymous author clearly intended no irony in this statement). Poe was dismissed as a "capital artist after the manner of Tennyson"; he was at best an imitator, and at the worst a plagiarist. In a letter to James Russell Lowell (who was not mentioned in the article), Poe named Charles Dickens as the author, but Lowell thought it by Dickens's friend John Forster, perhaps with some help by Dickens: "Forster is a friend of some of the Longfellow clique here which perhaps accounts for his putting L. at the top of our Parnassus."

It seems probable that Poe had this article festering in his mind when he reviewed Longfellow's anthology, *The Waif.* He started disarmingly enough. The "Proem" by the editor was the best poem in the book. Then he charged that an eight-line poem by a very minor versifier in the Longfellow circle (James Aldrich's "A Death-Bed") had such remarkable similarities with Thomas Hood's "The Death-Bed" that *somebody is a thief.*" More important, the *Waif* was "infected with a *moral taint* . . . a very careful avoidance of all American poets who may be supposed especially to interfere with the claims of Mr. Longfellow. These men Mr. Longfellow can continuously *imitate* (is that the word?) and yet never even incidentally commend."[21]

The "sting in the tail" of this review drew a hot reply from "H." (George S. Hillard, a close friend of Longfellow's), who claimed that an anthologist had the right of selecting poems that he liked, and that the charges of imitation, since they were patently false, needed no rejoinder. Poe added a temperate postscript to the letter, and here the matter might have ended if an anonymous scholar, signing himself "Pi Kappa Rho," had not noticed that what purported to be a Longfellow translation of a German poem by O. L. B. Wolff was, in fact, almost identical with a Scottish ballad by William Motherwell. The accusation started a minor literary storm, since Longfellow (averse to controversy of any kind) was very slow in saying that he had found the poem in a German anthology which did not indicate that the poem was a translation of a translation. In the meantime another Longfellow friend (now known to be Charles Sumner) defended the anthology on the ground that it was meant only for "the waifs and *estrays* of literature, which automatically excluded such established poets as Lowell and Bryant."

Poe returned to the attack, although indirectly. In an article, "Imitation—Plagiarism," he admitted that British accusations of American imitation were "undoubtedly well based." If not justified, this was explainable. The lack of an international copyright law made it impossible "for our men of genius to obtain remuneration for their labors.

They were forced into literary drudgery in order to make a living. The only writers who had the leisure for strictly literary tasks were "from the class of dilettanti"—many of them gifted, but "embued with a spirit of conservation, which is merely a mood of the imitative spirit." Such men were likely to be conscious or unconscious plagiarists, even though the sin of plagiarism involves the "quintessence of meanness," for when "a plagiarism is detected, it generally happens that the public sympathy is with the plagiarist, and his friends proceed to every extreme in the way of exculpation. But how unjust! We should sympathize rather with him upon whom the plagiarism has been committed. Not only is he robbed of his property—of his fame . . . but he is rendered liable by the crime of *the plagiarist to the suspicion of being a plagiarist himself.*

In his New York Historical Society lecture on the poets of America, Poe said that Longfellow had more genius than any other American poet, but that "his fatal alacrity at imitation made him borrow, when he had better at home." Poe felt that the most important part of his lecture was the attack on the prevailing "system of indiscriminate laudation of American books—a system which, more than any other one thing in the world, had tended to the depression of 'American literature' whose elevation it was designed to effect." But it was the comments on Longfellow by another friend, who wrote under the pseudonym of Outis (Greek for Nobody; probably Cornelius C. Felton) that provoked an unrestrained literary violence. Outis argued that there might be "identities" between poems without any plagiarism being involved on either side. In ´defending Longfellow, Outis suggested in a sophistical and rhetorical question that Poe was not quite innocent:

Who, for example, would wish to be guilty of the littleness of detracting from the uncommon merit of that remarkable

poem of . . . Mr. Poe's . . . entitled "The Raven," by charging
him with the paltriness of imitation? And yet, some snarling
critic, who might envy the reputation he had not the genius
to secure for himself, might refer to the frequent, very forcible,
but rather quaint repetition . . . as a palpable imitation of . . .
the Ancient Mariner.

He also pointed out eighteen similarities between "The
Raven" and an unpublished poem "The Bird of the
Dream," from which he printed a few extracts.[22]

Poe replied in a series of five articles in his own right
and without editorial anonymity. In the articles he re-
published most of the original documents. He began by
republishing the final paragraph of the *Waif* review, and
the two poems by Hood and Aldrich, and reiterated that
there were close similarities in a poem of sixteen lines and
one of eight lines. He then reprinted in full the letter of
Outis on plagiarism, disagreeing especially with the statement that charges of plagiarism "are perfectly absurd."
This Poe denied. The exposure of plagiarism was, or
could be, motivated by a strictly honorable attitude: by
the desire to defend the innocent victim against the thief.
Moreover, plagiarism does exist, in spite of Outis's denial,
and it is the duty of the critic to point it out. With good
reason, Poe objected to the manner and the method of his
opponent.

When by innuendo Outis suggested that Poe was a
plagiarist, he seemed to assume that this proved Longfellow and Aldrich original. When he himself had levied
charges, Poe had printed all the poems in full, giving
readers the chance to judge his arguments; Outis, in his
"design to impose the idea of similarity between my lines
and those of Coleridge," re-arranged the lines of "The
Ancient Mariner" and failed to note signficant differences:

Coleridge's lines are arranged in quatrains—mine in couplets.
His first and third lines rhyme at the close of the second and

fourth feet—mine flow continuously, without rhyme. His metre, briefly defined, is alternately tetrameter acatalectic and trimeter acatalectic—mine is uniformly octameter catalectic. It might be expected, however, that at least the *rhythm* would prove to be identical—but not so. Coleridge's is iambic (varied in the third foot of the first line with an anapaest)—mine is the exact converse, trochaic. The fact is, that neither in rhythm, metre, stanza, or rhyme, is there even a *single* point of *approximation* throughout;

The charge that there were eighteen similarities between "The Raven" and the unpublished "Bird of the Dream" seemed equally absurd. On the basis of the extracts printed, Poe demonstrated that sixteen were not similarities but dissimilarities; the two that were sustained show that in both poems there is "an allusion to the departed" and "a bird." But even granted that Outis had proved his case and that the resemblances existed,

He had clearly forgotten that the *mere* number of such coincidences proves nothing, because at any moment we can oblige it to prove too much. It is the easiest thing imaginable to suggest—and even to do that which Outis has failed in doing—to demonstrate a practically infinite series of identities between any two compositions in the world—but it by no means follows that all compositions in the world have a *similarity* one with the other, in any comprehensible sense of the term. I mean to say that regard must be had not *only* to the number of the coincidences, but to the peculiarity of each—this peculiarity growing less and less necessary, and the effect of number more and more important, in a ratio prodigiously accumulative, as the investigation progresses. And again—regard must be had not only to the number *and* peculiarity of the coincidences, but to the antagonistic differences, if any, which surround them—and very especially to *the space* over which the coincidences are spread, and the number or paucity of the events, or incidents, from among which the coincidences are selected. When Outis, for example, picks out his eighteen coincidences (which I am now granting as sustained) from a poem so long as The Raven, in collation with a poem not forthcoming, and

which may therefore, for anything anybody knows to the contrary, be as long as an infinite flock of ravens, he is merely
putting himself to unnecessary trouble in getting together
phantoms of arguments that can have no substance wherewith
to aid his demonstration, until the ascertained extent of the
unknown poem from which they are culled, affords them a
purpose and a palpability. Can any man doubt that between
The Iliad and the Paradise Lost there might be established
even a thousand very idiosyncratic identities?—and yet is any
man fool enough to maintain that the Iliad is the only original
of the Paradise Lost?

Outis had based his accusations only on unsupported
generalizations or upon twisted, unsatisfactory evidence;
Poe asserted proudly that "no man can point to a single
critique, among the very numerous ones which I have
written during the last ten years, which is either wholly
fault-finding or wholly in approbation; nor is there an
instance to be discovered, among all that I have published, of my having set forth, either in praise or censure,
a single opinion upon any critical topic of moment, without attempting, at least, to give it authority by something
that wore the semblance of a reason." Unfortunately, Poe
did not stop there. He again reprinted the Longfellow
and Tennyson poems on the death of the old year, and
repeated that Longfellow's imitation belonged to "the most
barbarous class of literary piracy"; he printed the Motherwell ballad and Longfellow's translation from Wolff, and
indicated that Longfellow's defense was really no defense
at all, since the German version had appeared in a book
clearly labelled as translations. To further bolster his case,
Poe unwisely declared that Longfellow in his *Spanish Student* had taken one scene from his own drama, *Politian.*
He pointed out similarities, noting that the "coincidences
here are too markedly peculiar to be gainsayed," although
in fact all of them seem to belong to the commonplaces of
drama. Poe felt that he had, in fact, been too lenient

rather than too harsh: "Had I accused him, in loud terms, of manifest and continued plagiarism, I should but have echoed the sentiment of every man of letters in the land beyond the immediate influence of the Longfellow *coterie*."

As his fellow-editor Charles F. Briggs noted, Poe's "very ticklish hobby" of insisting on plagiarism had hurt rather than helped his reputation. Belatedly Poe seems to have realized this. In a fifth article which is mainly a postscript to the earlier ones, he disclaimed any personal animus, malevolence, or discourtesy; he had brought no charge of moral delinquency against Longfellow or Aldrich, although if "in the heat of argument, I may have uttered any words which may admit of being tortured into such an interpretation, I here fully disclaim them on the spot." In this cooler and saner mood, he presented a quite different interpretation of imitation:

It appears to me that what seems to be the gross *inconsistency* of plagiarism as perpetrated by a poet, is very easily thus resolved:—the poetic sentiment (even without reference to the poetic power) implies a peculiarly, perhaps abnormally keen appreciation of the beautiful, with a longing for its assimilation, or absorption, into poetic identity. What the poet intensely admires, becomes thus, in very fact, although only partially, a portion of his own intellect. It has a secondary origination within his own soul—an origination altogether apart, although springing from its primary origination from without. The poet is thus possessed by another's thought, and cannot be said to take of it, possession. But, in either view, he thoroughly feels it as *his own*—and this feeling is counteracted only by the sensible presence of its true, palpable origin in the volume from which he has derived it—an origin which, in the long lapse of years it is almost impossible *not* to forget—for in the meantime the thought itself is forgotten. But the frailest association will regenerate it—it springs up with all the vigor of a new birth—its absolute originality is not even a matter of suspicion—and when the poet has written it and printed it,

and on its account is charged with plagiarism, there will be no
one in the world more entirely astounded than himself. Now
from what I have said it will be evident that the liability to
accidents of this character is in the direct ratio of the poetic
sentiment—of the susceptibility to the poetic impression; and
in fact all literary history demonstrates that, for the most
frequent and palpable plagiarisms, we must search the works
of the most eminent poets.[23]

*   *   *

For all his claims of originality, the influences of several
poets are evident in Poe's work. In *Tamerlane* there are
obvious traces and echoes of Byron's works; in *Politian*
there is even more direct evidence of the influence of
Manfred. The marks of Byron and of Tom Moore are also
pervasive in Poe's early lyrics. Although these influences
soon waned, they never entirely disappeared.

Of the older Romantic poets, Coleridge, Shelley, and
Keats had succeeded best in attaining a pure ideality. I
agree with Floyd Stovall that to Coleridge Poe was chiefly
indebted in youth for his literary thought, his critical
ideas, and much of his poetry, although he gradually absorbed these beliefs into his philosophy of literature.
Shelley's verse was unpremeditated. "If ever poet sang—
as a bird sings—earnestly—impulsively—with utter aban-
donment—to himself solely—and for the mere joy of his
own song—that poet was the author of 'The Sensitive
Plant.' Of Art—beyond that which is instinctive with
Genius—he either had little or disdained all." But he had
no affectations, and he was profoundly original.[24]

Poe felt more completely in tune with poets who were
more exactly his contemporaries, especially with Alfred
Tennyson and Elizabeth Barrett (after September, 1846,

Mrs. Robert Browning). A typical judgment he stated many times with slight variations: "I am not sure that Tennyson was not the greatest of poets. The uncertainty attending the public conception of the term 'poet' alone prevents me from proving that he is. Other bards produce effects which are, now and then, otherwise produced than by what we call poems; but Tennyson has produced an effect which only poetry does. . . . By the enjoyment or non-enjoyment of the 'Morte D'Arthur,' or of the 'Oenone,' I would test any one's ideal sense." In his final lecture, "The Poetic Principle," he stated flatly that he regarded Tennyson as "the noblest poet that ever lived."

The ideal poet would unite in one person the Shelleyan *abandon* and the Tennysonian poetic sense, with "the most profound Art (based both in Instinct and *Analysis*) and the sternest Will properly to blend and rigorously to control all."[25] For a time he thought that Elizabeth Barrett had succeeded. Certainly she was "the greatest—the most glorious of her sex," and to her he dedicated his 1845 *Raven and Other Poems*. But she deserved comparison with the best of poets, regardless of sex, as Poe indicated when he wrote that "With the exception of Tennyson's 'Locksley Hall,' I have never read a poem combining so much of the fiercest passion with so much of the most delicate imagination, as the 'Lady Geraldine's Courtship' of Miss Barrett" (1845).[26]

At least in part, Poe tended to judge other poets by the melodic effects which they imparted to their lines. As early as 1835, he noted that few persons were agreed on a proper versification or metre, and could only assign as a reason that music is a most indefinite conception. He studied prosody, with the result that the love of discords grew upon him, at the expense of a technically flawless harmony, and he prided himself "upon the accuracy of my ear." He continued his experiments with prosody, de-

fining verse as including rhythm, rhyme, metre and versification, and he soon came to the conclusion that little of
value had been written on English prosody. The principle
of verse should be related to that of another art; when this
is done, we realize that "The perception of pleasure in the
equality of *sounds* is the principle of *Music*." Unpracticed
ears can appreciate only simple equalities, but practiced
ears can appreciate the complexity of two or more simple
sounds conjointly. In verse, an inferior music, there is
less chance for complexity.

Nonetheless, the prosody of words is likewise founded
on equality, although with word-sounds that equality must
always be proximate rather than absolute. This is the
principle. Its application through scansion has only two
purposes: by the voice, to the ear only; by the written
symbol, to address the ear through the eye: "In either case
the object is the distinct marking of the rhythmical, musical, or reading flow. There *can* be no other object and
there is none." The written scansion is good only when it
truly represents the rhythm or music in the line; then it
exactly conveys the rhythm.

Poe admitted that most lines in English verse could be
scanned with the five regular feet (iambic, trochaic, ana-
pestic, dactylic, and spondee), with the addition of the
caesura, which he somewhat capriciously defined as "a
single *long syllable; but the length of this syllable varies*."
But this older method, while usable, has never been completely satisfactory. There are too many musical lines that
do not yield to conventional scansion. This can be done
only by admitting into our scansion the existence of a
bastard iambus or a bastard anapest or dactyl, differing
from the true foot "only in the *distribution* of this time.
The time, for example, occupied by the one short (or
half of long) syllable, in the ordinary iambus, is, in the
bastard, spread equally over two syllables, which are ac-

cordingly the *fourth of long.*" By this system, the principle of equality would be preserved.

To obviate the complication and the difficulty, Poe proposed a new method of scansion that would give to the eye the exact relative value of every syllable employed in verse:

I have already shown that enunciation, or *length,* is the point from which we start. In other words, we begin with a *long syllable.* This then is our unit; and there will be no need of accenting it at all. An unaccented syllable, in a system of accentuation, is to be regarded always as a long syllable. Thus a spondee would be without accent. In an iambus, the first syllable being "short," or the *half* of long, should be accented with a small 2, placed *beneath* the syllable; the last syllable, being long, should be unaccented;—the whole would be thus (control.) In a trochee, these accents would be merely con-

2

versed, thus (manly.) In a dactyl, each of the two final sylla-

2

bles, being the half of long, should, also, be accented with a small 2 beneath the syllable; and, the first syllable left unaccented, the whole would be thus (happiness.) In an anapaest

2 2

we should converse the dactyl thus, (in the land.) In the

2 2

bastard dactyl, each of the three concluding syllables being the *third* of long, should be accented with a small 3 beneath the syllable and the whole foot would stand thus, (flowers ever.) In

3 3 3

the bastard anapaest we should converse the bastard dactyle thus, (in the rebound.) In the bastard iambus, each of the

3 3 3

two initial syllables, being the fourth of long, should be accented, below with a small 4; the whole foot would be thus, (in the rain.) In the bastard trochee, we should converse the

4 4

bastard iambus thus, (many a.) In the quick trochee, each of

4 4

the three concluding syllables, being the *sixth* of long, should be accented, below, with a small 6; the whole foot would be

thus, (many are the.) The quick iambus is not yet created, and
most probably never will be, for it will be excessively useless,
awkward, and liable to misconception—as I have already shown
that even the quick trochee is:—but, should it appear, we must
accent it by conversing the quick trochee. The caesura, being
variable in length, but always *longer than "long,"* should be
accented, *above,* with a number expressing the length, or value,
of the distinctive foot of the rhythm in which it occurs. Thus
a caesura, occuring in a spondaic rhythm, would be accented
with a small 2 above the syllable, or, rather, foot. Occurring in
a dactylic or anapaestic rhythm, we also accent it with the 2,
above the foot. Occurring in an iambic rhythm, however, it
must be accented, above, with $1\frac{1}{2}$; for this is the relative value
of the iambus. Occurring in the trochaic rhythm, we give it, of
course, the same accentuation. For the complex $1\frac{1}{2}$, however,
it would be advisable to substitute the simpler expression $3/2$
which amounts to the same thing.

This system is in itself far more difficult and complex
than the conventional one; for that reason, it has never
been generally used. But the concept behind Poe's arguments have been largely adopted by a good many English
and American poets. He was advocating the loosening up
of the technique of versification by allowing for greater
variety within the poetic foot, and for making the poetic
foot at least approximately equal to a bar of music.[27]
In "the Raven," Poe made, as he had indicated, a conscious effort to put his theory of musicality into his rhythm
and metre. Some later writers have regarded his essay,
"The Philosophy of Composition," as an elaborate hoax.
Certainly it does not fully explain the genesis of the poem,
and the author glides over the fact that he was working on
it for two or three years before he published it. Yet everything in the essay fits into Poe's theories as he had stated
them in various scattered reviews.
He began with the *effect* that the poem would have.
Steadily he had insisted that while the poetic sentiment

might be feeling, the written poem was not, and should not be judged as, self-expression. The test of the poem was its ability to arouse that sentiment in readers. For this unity of effect, the reader must be able to complete the poem at one sitting; for this purpose, the ideal length was approximately one hundred lines. "The Raven" runs to one hundred and eight. Since the sole legitimate province of the poem is beauty and its end pleasure, these would be the province of the poem, for Poe firmly believed that the "pleasure which is at once the most intense, the most elevating and the most pure is, I believe, found in the contemplation of the beautiful." In life, Truth, or the satisfaction of the intellect, and Passion, or the satisfaction of the heart, were of equal importance, but in poetry they could only aid the general effect by elucidation or contrast, as discords do in music. What he desired was the excitement or pleasurable elevation of the soul, and this could be achieved only through beauty, and its highest manifestation was sadness: "Melancholy is thus the most legitimate of all poetical tones."

The length, the province, and the tone being determined, Poe considered various specific devices. One way to secure musicality was through the refrain, and he determined to use the single word "nevermore" at the close of each stanza, but to give it freshness by the variation of its application. A raven—"the bird of ill omen"—was to repeat the single ominous and sonorous word, about the most melancholy of all poetical subjects: the death of a beautiful woman. The poem took somewhat the form of a debate, the lover lamenting his deceased mistress and the raven destroying his hopes with the repeated "nevermore." Although Poe does not directly make the point, it is difficult not to interpret the raven as the man's conscience, and the poem as a debate between the man and his personified conscience.

In this essay and in several of the later reviews, Poe presents his final theory about the interaction of the imagination and the reason. No longer is the genesis of the poem in the imagination, and the artistry in the execution. Instead, the two work together concurrently, simultaneously. The form dictates the idea as much as the idea dictates the form. They are inseparable.

He sought originality, not in rhythm or metre, but by the combination of lines into stanzas; he sought to give an added unity by a close circumscription of place (a single room); he sought to give greater richness and complexity to the whole, by adding an under-current of meaning that would make the raven a debate between a man and his conscience.

There is hardly an idea or a concept in the essay that Poe had not stated before. Here he simply gathered together in one place the ideas that, when scattered, had aroused little or no protest, and applied them specifically to his most popular poem. This conjunction leads many readers to feel that Poe wrote artificially and mechanically, or on the other hand that he was indulging in pseudo-analysis. Certainly the analysis was written after the creation. But Poe was a conscious artist, perhaps interested in explaining to himself as well as to his readers the process through which a finished work of art is formed. It is not by accident that "The Philosophy of Composition" was to become to other conscious artists, especially to French poets, critics, and even musical composers, a guiding light. In the words of Maurice Ravel, "To me the finest treatise on composition, certainly the one that has influenced me most, is Poe's essay on the genesis of a poem."[28]

In attempting to round up and give cohesion to his often-stated but scattered theories in "The Poetic Principle," Poe necessarily reiterated many of his earlier ideas, often with little change in wording. He continued to

maintain that a long poem was a contradiction in terms
and that *Paradise Lost* was poetical only when viewed as
a series of minor poems; that a true poem deserved its title
only when it elevated the soul and that all psychal excite-
ments are of necessity transient; that unity is a vital requisite in all works of art; that length is no criterion of excellence, but that undue brevity degenerates into mere
epigrammatism and never produces a profound or lasting
impression; and that ideality is a requisite in the best
poems. Again he deplored what he continued to call the
"heresy of *The Didactic*," as having "accomplished more
in the corruption of our poetical literature than all its
other enemies combined." This arose from a misunder-
standing of the functions of the mind as related to life. The
intellect concerns itself with truth; taste informs us of the
beautiful; the moral sense is regardful of duty. Taste wages
war "upon Vice solely on the ground of her deformity, her
disproportion—her animosity to the fitting, to the appropriate, to the harmonious—in a word, to Beauty." But
the mere repetition of known earthly beauties, however
glowingly or skillfully done, is not poetry, at least in the
highest sense. The poet must strive for something more,
even while knowing that he can never fully attain it. He
must make a wild effort to reach the beauty above, to ap-
prehend and express the supernal loveliness which has
given to us the poetic sentiment.

This principle or sentiment can be expressed in any
art-form, perhaps best in music; it can even be felt but not
expressed. When expressed in words, with the aid of
music, it becomes poetry:

—I would define, in brief, the Poetry of words as *The Rhythmical Creation of Beauty*. Its sole arbiter is Taste. With the
Intellect or with the Conscience, it has only collateral relations. Unless incidentally, it has no concern whatever either
with Duty or with Truth.

A few words, however, in explanation. *That* pleasure which is at once the most pure, the most elevating, and the most intense, is derived, I maintain, from the contemplation of the Beautiful. In the contemplation of Beauty we alone find it possible to attain that pleasurable elevation, or excitement, *of the soul,* which we recognise as the Poetic Sentiment, and which is so easily distinguished from Truth, which is the satisfaction of the Reason, or from Passion, which is the excitement of the heart. I make Beauty, therefore—using the word as inclusive of the sublime—I make Beauty the province of the poem, simply because it is an obvious rule of Art that effects should be made to spring as directly as possible from their causes:—no one as yet having been weak enough to deny that the peculiar elevation in question is at least *most readily* attainable in the poem. It by no means follows, however, that the incitements of Passion, or the precepts of Duty, or even the lessons of Truth, may not be introduced into a poem, and with advantage; for they may subserve, incidentally, in various ways, the general purposes of the work:—but the true artist will always contrive to tone them down in proper subjection to that *Beauty* which is the atmosphere and the real essence of the poem.[29]

Beyond any question, Poe unduly narrows the field of poetry and the domain of literature. As his definition clearly indicates, he was interested in a poetry of mood and of tone, not of intellect. He was fundamentally interested only in lyric poetry. He has been accused of critical rationalization on the ground that this was the only kind of poetry which he could write, and that his theoretic principles were used to justify his creative limitations. There is no doubt some truth in this. If so, the sin has not been exclusively Poe's. As Henry Timrod noted, theories propounded by poets "seldom attain a greater breadth than suffices to shelter the theorist and the models from which he has drawn his arguments and his inspiration." There seems no reason to believe that Poe, however narrow or misguided he may have been, was not honest in his belief that poetic tension was preferable to extension, and that only the lyric deserved the name of poem.

There is another contributing factor. It must not be forgotten that in poetry and in fiction Poe gained his highest popularity through magazine, not through book, publication, and that throughout his mature life his steady ambition was to found and edit a distinguished, independent magazine. To him, lyric poetry was ideally suited for magazine publication; epic and dramatic and even narrative poetry was not. He assured John Pendleton Kennedy as to fiction and Henry Wadsworth Longfellow as to poetry that their work would appear to greater advantage in his projected *Penn Magazine* than it would in book form. His motive was in part personal and selfish, but there is conclusive evidence that he believed what he wrote. The "tendency of the age" was in the direction of magazine literature; Poe might have noted, but did not, that he was himself as writer and editor largely responsible in this country for this new type of literature. In taste and in thought, Poe belonged almost exclusively to his own century; he was excited by the emergence of a new medium for the publication of certain types of writing: specifically, for the tale and the lyric poem. His theories of poetry fit the capabilities of this new medium almost perfectly. Whether consciously or subconsciously, he slowly evolved an aesthetic for a magazine literature.

A Summing Up

Poe's weaknesses as critic are in the main obvious. Perhaps the least important and the least pleasant is his propensity for personal ridicule. It is relatively easy to pardon his comments in 1831 on William Wordsworth and Samuel Johnson because of Poe's youth; it is not so easy to accept the descent into personalities in the 1836 reviews of novels by Theodore S. Fay and William Gilmore Simms. The reasons behind his sneering attacks on William Ellery Channing the younger, W. W. Lord, and Rufus Dawes are more complex, arising out of dislike of Transcendentalism in general as well as personal dislike, pique, and probably jealousy.[1] Even so, the critic buttresses his case against the three poets with pertinent quotations and telling analyses, but he disregarded the probability, if not indeed the fact (which he proclaimed elsewhere), that the objective treatments would have been more devastating without the personal ridicule. Poe desired an analytical criticism, but he did not always succeed in achieving it himself.

Yet, when one compares his criticism with that of some of his journalistic enemies (the Clarks, Griswold, English, Outis, and others), Poe seems almost restrained. It was a period of cutthroat criticism, under the rules that might govern a street brawl rather than a duel. It is not surprising that Poe often substituted the sneer or the virulent attack on the man for a reasoned analysis of the work. He was a practicing journalist and he was fighting to survive personally and financially.

A weakness that is basically the reverse side of the same coin is his tendency to overpraise the works of his friends, especially the feminine poets. Of Frances S. Osgood he wrote that "in no one poetical requisite is she deficient." She was not the equal of Maria Brooks in imagination and vigor, or of Amelia Welby in "passionate tenderness and rhythmical skill," but in that charm which "we are accustomed to designate as *grace,* she is absolutely without a rival, we think, either in our own country or in England." He thought Elizabeth Oakes Smith's "The Sinless Child" had "the lofty merit of originality," and that Estelle Anna Lewis's "The Forsaken" was *"inexpressibly beautiful."* Although he noted that he could not point an arrow at any woman, he often erred in the other direction: his praise occasionally seems fulsome and strained.[2]

This was a human and appealing weakness. It is less easy to understand Poe's almost psychopathic obsession with plagiarism and imitation. Literature, like humanistic thought, is a continuum. Poe at times seemed to realize this elementary truth, as when he wrote that only God has truly created and the artist can only present in novel combinations what already is. Too, some of the men he attacked, especially Longfellow, were indeed vulnerable on the charge of imitation. Other attacks, like the accusation that Hawthorne's "Howe's Masquerade" was "a very flattering coincidence of thought" which resembled plagiarism of his "William Wilson," were based on ignorance; Poe was not aware that Hawthorne's story was published earlier than his own.[3] Generally, however, it was his perverse idea that the spirit of imitativeness constituted plagiarism which aroused heated and frequently justified attacks on his critical judgment.

Although it earned him no personal enmity, a more serious restriction on the validity of Poe's critical theory and his specific evaluations is clearly traceable to his restricted knowledge. He knew the Bible and Shakspeare thoroughly, but he had little appreciation or knowledge of Greek literature, although considerably more of Roman. He gained much as a poet from his study of Milton, yet he rarely admitted the scope of Milton's poetic ability. In more ways than by the dates of birth and death he was a child of the nineteenth-century, of the romantic movement. In poetry his chief sources of literary inspiration were Coleridge, Byron, Moore, Shelley, Keats, and Tennyson; in fiction, the Gothic school of tale-tellers; in criticism, Coleridge and A. W. von Schlegel.

This means that Poe unduly narrowed the domain of literature. He would admit only a few types of lyric poetry to be poetry. Although epic, dramatic, philosophical, and narrative poems might arouse interest and have literary value, they were not the values of poetry but of something akin to prose—at best, of verse. Only the indefinite poem not directly concerned with moral issues could be truly beautiful; only the relatively short poem could have totality of effect.

Yet this narrowed intensity gives character and strength to his criticism. In a time of literary backscratching and headbashing, he sought to achieve an honest, fearless, independent criticism, based upon international rather than personal or national standards. With a few notable exceptions, he succeeded in this aim. He objected to what he called the cant of generality, and demanded a firm textual analysis as the basis of judgment. Sometimes this led to undue quibbling, but in general it gives a firm understanding to the reader of the point Poe is making. Even when alleging what today seems unjustifiable charges of plagiarism, Poe was scrupulous about presenting his evidence. As he noted in his reply to Outis, Poe had printed in full both Tennyson's and Longfellow's poems: at least the reader had a chance to judge whether or not the accusation was justified.

Although his consistent attacks on the heresy of the didactic were overdone and overwrought, Poe was aesthetically sound when he objected to an explicit moral. Once again, he unduly narrowed the domain of poetry when he attempted to rule out ethical and philosophical works as outside the scope of poetic art; Henry Timrod answered him effectively and persuasively in contending that beauty, truth, and power were all constituents of great poetry. This partially invalidates Poe's theory, but not completely. His desire for an absolute unity in a poem or tale led inevitably to his belief that the entire work should be the communication. A moral might be implicit, but it must stay under the surface; when it was made explicitly or tacked on at the end, not only did the work suffer artistically but the writer revealed his own defects and deficiences as an artist.

As a writer, Poe drew upon his own experiences and obsessions, much more than on his observations. At least twice in his adult life he teetered on the thin edge between sanity and insanity; it is not by accident that his finest stories and poems are analyses of obsessed minds. Yet there is also the constant desire for a supernal beauty, for something that would lift man's spirit above his body and beyond this earth.

This is one phase of Poe's work, and a motivating force in his theory. Yet there was a basic dichotomy which he reconciled. He was, as he wrote of himself, essentially a magazinist; he was an excellent editor; he tried repeatedly to establish an ideal magazine. He molded his own creative work into this structure; he evolved his critical theories through magazine reviews and articles. His practice conformed with his theories, not through rationalization because of his inability to write long works but because he was interested both in an ideal unity and in works suitable for magazines. Quite consciously, he worked out an aesthetic for a magazine literature.

Notes

I. INTRODUCTION

[1]"Marginalia," in *Complete Works of Edgar Allan Poe*, edited by James A. Harrison, New York, 1902, 17 volumes (hereafter cited as *Works*), XVI, 82; *The Letters of Edgar Allan Poe*, edited by John Ward Ostrom, Cambridge, Mass., 1948, 2 volumes (hereafter cited as *Letters*), I, 270; I, 162-70. On Poe and the South, see Jay B. Hubbell's "Poe and the Southern Literary Tradition," in *Texas Studies in Literature and Language*, II (Summer, 1960), 151-71, and his *The South in American Literature*, Durham, 1954, 528-50. Although this work was almost completed before Richard Beale Davis's *Intellectual Life in Jefferson's Virginia* was published (Chapel Hill, 1964), I have found it useful. Of value also is Killis Campbell's *The Mind of Poe*, Cambridge, Mass., 1933 (reprinted New York, 1962), and "Poe's Reading," University of Texas *Studies in English*, V, (Oct., 1925), 166-96.

[2]Margaret Alterton, *Origins of Poe's Critical Theory*, Iowa City, 1925; Alterton and Craig (editors), *Edgar Allan Poe*, New York, 1935, XXXIII-IV; lii-liv. For an excellent discussion, see Emerson R. Marks, "Poe as Literary Theorist," *American Literature*, 33 (Nov., 1961), 296-306, and Edmund Wilson, "Poe as a Literary Critic," *Nation*, CLV (Oct. 31, 1942), 452-53.

[3]For a careful examination of Poe's critical writings, see William Doyle Hull, "A Canon of the Critical Works of Edgar Allan Poe" (Univ. of Virginia dissertation, 1941). Since I agree that they were not by Poe, I have disregarded the perfunctory review of Bryant's Poems, Manzoni's *I Promessi Sposi*, and Irving's *Crayon Miscellany*, No. II, all reprinted in VIII, *Works*. Still extremely useful are The Introductions to F. C. Prescott's *Selections from the Critical Writings of Edgar Allan Poe*, New York, 1909, and John B. Moore's *Selections from Poe's Literary Criticism*, New York, 1926.

[4]In "Al Aaraaf," II, 47, Poe has an excellent example of the deliberate confusion of the senses, in a man who "sees the darkness coming as a cloud—Is not its form—its voice—most palpable and loud?" This was evidently based on personal experience, for Poe wrote of himself directly

that "I have often thought I could distinctly hear the sound of darkness as it stole over the horizon." The color symbolism in "The Masque of the Red Death" and in other stories rather indicates, although evasively, that Poe in his youth may have seen people as colors, or associated certain colors with certain individuals. He also noted that the "orange ray of the spectrum and the buzz of a gnat (which never rises above the second A) affect me with nearly similar sensations. In hearing the gnat, I perceive the color. In perceiving the color, I seem to hear the gnat" (XVI, 17-18). He believed, too, that "odors have an altogether peculiar force, in affecting us through association" (XVI, 31). He was fond of association phrases like the "grey rumble of the dawn" and the "yellow cry of the beetles."

On Poe's influence in France, see Patrick F. Guinn, *The French Face of Poe*, Carbondale, 1937; C. P. Cambiaire, *The Influence of Edgar Allan Poe in France*, New York, 1927; Lois and Francis E. Hyslop, Jr., editors, *Baudelaire on Poe*, State College, Pa., 1952; and Haldeen Braddy, *Glorious Incense*, Washington, 1953, 98-149.

I. POE AS A MAGAZINE CRITIC

1Floyd Stovall, "An Interpretation of Poe's 'Al Aaraaf,'" University of Texas *Studies in English*, IX, 106-33.

2*Works*, VII: xxxv-xlii; VIII: 275-79. Poe re-phrased this attack and added to it in "The Exordium" (*Graham's Magazine*, Jan. 1842; *Works*, XI, 1-2): "Time was when we imported our critical decisions from the mother country. For many years we enacted a perfect farce of subserviency to the *dicta* of Great Britain. At last a revulsion of feeling, with self-disgust, necessarily ensued. Urged by these, we plunged into the opposite extreme. In throwing *totally* off that 'authority,' whose voice had so long been so sacred, we even surpassed, and by much, our original folly. But the watchword now was, 'A national literature!'—as if any true literature *could be* 'national'—as if the world at large were not the only proper stage for the literary *histrio*. We became suddenly, the merest and maddest *partizans* in letters. Our papers spoke of 'tariffs' and 'protection.' Our Magazines had habitual passages about that 'truly native novelist, Mr. Cooper,' or that 'staunch American genius, Mr. Paulding.' Unmindful of the spirit of the axioms that 'a prophet has not honor in his own land' and that 'a hero is never a hero to his *valet-de-chambre*'—axioms founded in reason and in truth—our reviews urged the propriety—our booksellers the necessity, of strictly 'American' themes. A foreign subject, at this epoch, was a weight more than enough to drag down into the very depths of critical damnation the finest writer owning nativity in the States; while, on the reverse, we found ourselves daily in the paradoxical dilemma of liking, or pretending to like, a stupid book the better because (sure enough) its stupidity was of our own growth, and discussed our own affairs."

3For William Wirt's influence, see Margaret Alterton, *Origins of Poe's Critical Theory*, 46 ff. However, Wirt's letter to a law student, published in *S L M*, I: 33, is not to Poe but to W. H. Miller (see J. B. Hubbell in *Eight American Authors*, 1956, 13-14, and R. B. Davis, "Poe and William Wirt," *American Literature* 16 (Nov., 1944, 212-20). Kennedy's letter is quoted in David K. Jackson's *Poe and the Southern Literary Messenger,* Richmond, 1934, 4-5. For Kennedy's assistance to Poe, see the index of Charles H. Bohner's *John Pendleton Kennedy: Gentleman from Baltimore,* Baltimore, 1961.

4Alterton, *op. cit.,* 7-8, 30-34; *Letters,* I: 77; *Works,* 3-5.

5Robert C. McLean, *George Tucker,* Chapel Hill, 1961, 139-43; Richard Beale Davis, *Intellectual Life in Jefferson's Virginia,* Chapel Hill, 1964, 258-59, 286-87. See also William A. Charvat, *Origins of American Critical Thought,* Philadelphia, 1936, and Robert D. Jacobs, "Poe's Heritage from Jefferson's Virginia" (Johns Hopkins dissertation, 1953).

6*Letters,* I, 100-02; *The Correspondence of Thomas Holley Chivers,* edited by Emma Lester Chase and Lois Ferry Parks, Providence, 1957, 10-12. Poe's protests here and later did not convince his kindly younger contemporary, John Esten Cooke, who called Poe the author of "some of the fiercest, most savage, and most unfair literary criticism ever written in America . . . . He searches for weak points in every writer, completely discarding, it would seem, the just maxim that true criticism is apprecia-tion" (John Esten Cooke, *Poe as a Literary Critic,* edited by N. B. Fagin, Baltimore, 1946, 1-2, 6).

7*Works,* XI, 3, 6-7; VIII, 9-10; VIII, 62, 72; VIII, 155-58, X, 126-31. Poe's own youthful carelessness about punctuation drew a protest from T. W. White, and Poe promised to "pay special attention to what you suggested in relation to the punctuation" (*Letters,* I, 63). However, his punctuation remained rhetorical rather than grammatical.

8*Works,* VIII, 280-303; IX, 145.

9A. H. Quinn, *Edgar Allan Poe,* New York, 1941, 259, 306; *Letters.* I, 141; II, 330: He wanted "a journal in which the men of genius may fight their battles, upon some terms of equality, with those dunces the men of talent."

10*Letters,* I, 141. Poe wrote that he had entered first into an engagement with *The New-York Review* and afterward with *Burton's Gentleman's Magazine* merely to keep his head above water "as regards money." See Quinn, 277-304; 263-66; *Letters,* I, 129-32, 137-39, 118-19; *Works,* XI, 3.

11*Letters,* I, 138-57; 175. He wrote to Kennedy (p. 150) that the "leading feature proposed is that of an absolutely independent criticism."

12*Letters,* I, 152, 154, 210, 212, 216; *Works,* XVI, 78-79: The disad-vantages of no copyright law "are these: First, we have injury to our national literature by repressing the efforts of our men of genius; for genius, as a general rule, is poor in worldly goods and cannot write for nothing. Our genius being thus repressed, we are written *at* only by our 'gentlemen of elegant leisure,' and mere gentlemen of elegant leisure have been noted, time out of mind, for the insipidity of their productions. In general, too, they are obstinately conservative, and this feeling leads them into imitation of foreign, more especially of British models. This is one main source of the imitativeness with which, as a people, we have been justly charged, although the first cause is to be found in our position as a colony. Colonies have always naturally aped the mother land.

"In the second place, irreparable ill is wrought by the almost exclusive dissemination among us of foreign—that is to say, of monarchical or aristocratical sentiment in foreign books; nor is this sentiment less fatal to democracy because it reaches the people themselves directly in the gilded pill of the poem or the novel.

"We have next to consider the impolicy of our committing, in the national character, an open and continuous wrong on the frivolous pretext of its benefiting ourselves.

"The last and by far the most important consideration of all, however, is that sense of insult and injury aroused in the whole active intellect of the world, the bitter and fatal resentment excited in the universal heart of literature—a resentment which will not and which cannot make nice distinctions between the temporary perpetrators of wrong and that democracy in general which permits its perpetration. The autorial body is the most autocratic on the face of the earth. How, then, can those institutions even hope to be safe which systematically persist in trampling it under foot?"

[13]Prospectus quoted in Quinn, 306-08; see also 316-20. *Letters,* I, 161-65 (quotation on 162) , 166-70; *Works,* XVI, 78-79.

[14]*Works,* VIII, 169-70; VII, 216; X, 152; X, 156.

[15]*Works,* X, 122,117, 40; XII, 151-53.

[16]*Works,* XVI, 81; XI, 1-2.

[17]*Works,* VIII, 51-52. For an excellent discussion of Poe's feud with the *knickerbocker* group, see Sidney P. Moss, *Poe's Literary Battles,* Durham, 1963, and Perry Miller, *The Raven and the Whale,* New York, 1956. The Transcendentalist tendency to over-praise Longfellow was in part leavened by the excellence of his work, but Poe could see no excuse for the praise of William Ellery Channing, whose poetry he thought ridiculous (*Works,* XIII, 169-70, and especially XI, 174-190; in this review Poe again stoops to personal ridicule, inventing a "Bobby Button" school of poetry to emphasize what he considered the absurdity of Channing's verse. The review is, however, somewhat redeemed by Poe's close textual analysis). On Bryant, Chivers quotes Poe as saying that he held "the policy,—or shall I call it politeness—to speak, in noticing Bryant's Poems, respectfully," although Bryant, admirable in many ways, did not understand the true nature of poetry and therefore "has never written the highest order of poetry" (*Chivers' Life of Poe,* edited by Richard Beale Davis, New York, 1952, 48-49) . For his favorable reviews of Bryant, see *Works,* IX, 268-305, and X, 85-91. In September, 1838, he declined to write an article-review of Irving's works because he would have to give "his entire works a reperusal," although he was tempted because "Irving is much over-rated, and a nice distinction might be drawn between his just and his surreptitious and adventitious reputation—between what is due to the pioneer solely, and what to the writer" (*Letters,* I, 111-12) . Poe also thought Irving too close an imitator of Addison. For the quotations on Hawthorne, see *Works,* XII, 141-42.

[18]*Works,* XI, 1-8. Poe thought that "even Macaulay's nearest approach to criticism in its legitimate sense" was in his article on Ranke's *History of the Popes,* but the end result of these generalized articles was "that criticism, being everything in the universe, is, consequently, nothing whatever in fact."

[19]*Works,* IX, 207-43; VII, 216. The italics are Poe's.

20*Letters*, II, 328. Poe added that readers think these stories "more ingenious than they are—on account of their method and *air* of method. In the 'Murders in the Rue Morgue,' for instance, where is the ingenuity of unravelling a web which you yourself (the author) have woven for the express purpose of unravelling? The reader is made to confound the ingenuity of the suppositious Dupin with that of the writer of the story." Rex Stout, creator of Nero Wolfe and Archie Goodwin, stressed the soundness of Poe's aesthetic theories in "Grim Fairy Tales," *Saturday Review of Literature*, xxxii (April 16, 1949), 30.

II. POE ON FICTION

1Quinn, 191-201, 745-46; Alterton, 7-45.

2*Works*, VIII, 146-47; *Southern Literary Messenger*, I (Feb., 1835), 315; *Works*, VIII, 32-37, 63-73. See also the Introduction by Cecil B. Williams to Bird's *Nick of the Woods*, New York, 1939, XX-XXI.

3*Works*, IX, 126-39; XV, 156, 203. He continued to think *Calavar* the best of Bird's novels, and "beyond doubt one of the best of American novels."

4*Works*, VIII, 4-11, XV, 155-84; *Letters*, I, 58-60.

5*Works*, VIII, 52. Poe's most cogent statement about his dislike of Prefaces appeared in his review of a non-fictional book, Alexander Slidell's *Spain Revisited* (*Works*, IX, 1-2): "With the *Dedicatory Letter* prefixed to *Spain Revisited*, we have no patience whatever. It does great credit to the kind and gentlemanly feelings of Lieutenant Slidell, but it forms no inconsiderable drawback upon our previously entertained opinions of his good taste. We can at no time, and under no circumstances, see either meaning or delicacy in parading the sacred relations of personal friendship before the unscrupulous eyes of the public. And even when these things are well done and briefly done, we do believe them to be in the estimation of all persons of nice feelings a nuisance and an abomination. But it very rarely happens that the closest scrutiny can discover in the least offensive of these dedications any thing better than extravagance, affectation or incongruity. We are not sure that it would be impossible, in the present instance, to designate gross examples of all three. What connection has the name of Lieutenant Upshur with the present Spanish Adventures of Lieutenant Slidell? None. Then why insist upon a connection which the world cannot perceive? The Dedicatory letter, in the present instance, is either a *bona fide* epistle actually addressed before publication to Lieutenant Upshur, intended strictly as a memorial of friendship, and published because no good reasons could be found for the non-publication—or its plentiful professions are all hollowness and falsity, and it was never meant to be any thing more than a very customary public compliment."

6*Works*, VIII, 51-62; *Letters*, I, 101-02. When he reviewed unfavorably Morris Mattson's *Paul Ulric* (*Works*, VIII, 178-205), Poe returned to the attack: "when we called Norman Leslie the silliest book in the world we had certainly never seen Paul Ulric." When he dealt with Fay in the articles on Autography, he stated, evidently with pride, that *Norman Leslie* "is more familiarly remembered as 'The Great Used Up'" (*Works*, XV, 174, 220). Poe considered Mattson a flagrant plagiarist of *Gil Blas*, of

Scott's *Anne of Geierstein,* and various others, but he reserved his biting irony for Mattson's wholesale borrowings from *The Curiosities of Literature;* Isaac D'Israeli was "one of the most scoundrelly plagiarists in Christendom. He had not scrupled to steal entire passages verbatim from Paul Ulric" (*Works,* VIII, 204) .

7*Works,* VIII, 143-58; *Letters,* I, 101. Poe felt that a novel should be self-contained (146-47) : "The interweaving of fact with fiction is at all times hazardous, and presupposes on the part of general readers that degree of intimate acquaintance with fact that should never be presupposed. In the present instance, the author has failed, so we think, in confining either his truth or his fable within its legitimate individual domain. Nor do we at all wonder at his failure in performing what no novelist whatever has hitherto performed."

8*Works,* X, 49-56; XII, 247-50; XIII, 93-97; XV, 168, 193; XVI, 41. Poe concluded this estimate in "Marginalia" by declaring that "leaving out of the question Brockden Brown and Hawthorne, (who are each a *genus,*) he is immeasurably the best writer of fiction in America. He has more vigor, more imagination, more movement and more general capacity than all our novelists (save Cooper) , combined."

9*Letters,* I, 94, 163, 165, 167, 169; *Works,* X, 96-99; XI, 205-220; XV, 108, 148, 206.

10*Works,* VIII, 94-100; 160-62; XV, 108-13, 205. Rather surprisingly, Poe has only mild praise for her stories and sketches (VIII, 160-62) .

11*Works,* IX, 243-65; XV, 195-96; XVI, 142, where he wrote that *George Balcombe* "is almost as good as 'Caleb Williams.' "

12*Letters,* I, 193; *Works,* IX, 106-16; XV, 188.

13*Works,* XI, 8-10. Harrison includes a review of Bulwer's *Zanoni* as by Poe (XI, 115-23) , but in *Letters,* I, 202, Poe requested Joseph Evans Snodgrass to publish a denial that he had written this "exceedingly ignorant and flippant review." Although Poe thought the imitator had made a mess of aping Poe's manner, the method and the tone indicate that Poe may have had a hand in it and was infuriated by editorial changes and revisions after he left *Graham's Magazine* (he claimed his last work appeared in May, 1842; the review appeared in June) . The reviewer makes a distinction between the novel and the romance that Poe would have agreed with: "A novel, in the true acceptation of the name, is a picture of real life. The plot may be involved, but it must not transcend probability. The agencies introduced must belong to real life. Such were Gil Blas and Tom Jones, confessedly the two best novels extant. Whether the title was properly applied, at the inception, is not the question. Usage and common sense have affixed a definite meaning to the word. When authors cease to paint real life they cease to write novels." Since Poe did not believe that a description or imitation of life was sufficient to make a true art, he naturally preferred the romance: "The mere imitation, however accurate, of what *is,* in Nature, entitles no man to the sacred name of 'Artist' " (*Works,* XVI, 164) .

14*Works,* VIII, 170: "Men do not look upon it in the light of a literary performance. Defoe has none of their thoughts—Robinson all."

15*Works,* VII, 229-34; VIII, 223.

¹⁶*Works*, IX, 168-69; X, 110-12; X, 160-62; X, 197-202; X, 214-20; XI, 10-11; XI, 85-98; XIV, 171.

¹⁷*Works*, X, 197; XI, 85, 90.

¹⁸*Works*, VIII, 222-29. Since *Rienzi* would be so widely read, Poe noted that "our usual custom of a digest of the narrative would be superfluous." For Mrs. Child, *Works*, IX, 146-55; quotation on 153.

¹⁹*Works*, X, 114-33; quotations on 116-17, 120-21, and 121-22. In the attempt to secure perfection of plot, Bulwer had sacrificed too much. There was a "continual and vexatious shifting of scene," and the author floundered "in the vain attempt to keep all his multitudinous incidents at one and the same moment before the eye." The reader barely had time to get interested in one scene before he was disconcertingly shifted to another.

²⁰*Works*, X, 132. The apparent contradictions in Bulwer's mind fascinated Poe (X, 212): "Mr. Bulwer is *never* lucid, and seldom profound. His intellect seems to be rather well balanced than lofty; rather comprehensive than penetrative. His taste is exquisite. His style, in its involution and obscurity, partakes of the involution of his thoughts. Apart from his mere intellect, however,—or rather as a portion of that intellect,—we recognize in his every written word the keenest appreciation of the right, the beautiful, and the true. Thus he is a man worthy of all reverence, and we do not hesitate to say that we look upon the charges of immoral tendency which have been so pertinaciously adduced against his fictions as absurdly *little* and untenable in the mass."

²¹*Works*, IX, 45-48 and XVI, 10-11, where it is called "a strangely pathetic and richly imaginative production, replete with the loftiest tragic power." On Stone, IX, 24-33; quotation on 48.

²²*Works*, IX, 205; X, 142-55. Poe objected that the title and method of publication gave a false appearance of unity to the book. The comparison is on 150.

²³*Works*, XI, 39-64, esp. 51-53; *Letters*, II, 328.

²⁴*Works*, X, 30-39. On 37, he noted that Fouqué's "plan is essentially distinct from Allegory, yet it has too close an affinity to that most indefensible species of writing." On XI, 247, he praises *Undine* because the moral is suggested, not stated, and calls the romance "that superb *poem*." On XIII, 149, again attacking allegory, Poe added that "properly handled, judiciously subdued, and making its nearest approach to truth in a not obtrusive and therefore not unpleasant *appositeness*, the 'Undine' of De La Motte Fouqué is the best, and undoubtedly a very remarkable specimen." Poe thought Eugene Sue's *Mysteries of Paris* a "work of unquestionable power . . . a paradox of childish folly and consummate skill"; and that Victor Hugo's *Notre-Dame de Paris* was a "fine example of the force which can be gained by concentration, or unity of place"—a device which he consciously employed in "The Raven," as described in "The Philosophy of Composition" (*Works*, XIV, 204): "it has always appeared to me that a close *circumscription of place* is absolutely necessary to the effect of insulated incident: it has the force of a frame to a picture."

²⁵*Letters*, I, 57-58, 77-78, 84. In the Preface to his *Tales of the Grotesque and Arabesque*, Poe justifiably protested that his "terror is not of Germany but of the soul" (*Works*, I, 150-51). For an interesting discus-

sion of Poe's own art, see Edward Wagenknecht, *Edgar Allan Poe,* New York, 1963, ch. 4, and Edward H. Davidson, *Poe: A Critical Study,* Cambridge, Mass., 1957.

[26] Review of *The Crayon Miscellany,* No. III, *Works,* VIII, 91-92 (I do not believe that the review of No. II, 40-41, is by Poe, but by E. V. Sparhawk). The *Astoria* review is in *Works,* IX, 207-43. On the tales and essays of Irving, XI, 102, 105, 110; XIII, 153-54; *Letters,* I, 121.

[27] *Works,* VIII, 257-65.

[28] *Works,* XIII, 153-54. See n. 26.

[29] *Works,* XI, 102-13; quotation on 113. Hawthorne's story had in fact been published earlier than Poe's.

[30] *Works,* XIII, 141-55, esp. 143, 147-48, 155. Poe overrated the originality of his own stories: "In writing these Tales one by one, at long intervals, I have kept the book-unity always in mind—that is, each has been composed with reference to its effect as part of *a whole.* In this view, one of my chief aims has been the widest diversity of subject, thought, & especially *tone* & manner of handling. Were all my tales now before me in a large volume and as the composition of another—the merit which would principally arrest my attention would be the wide *diversity and* variety. You will be surprised to hear me say that (omitting one or two of my first efforts) I do not consider any one of my stories *better* than another. There is a vast variety of kinds and, in degree of value, these kinds vary —but each tale is equally good *of its kind.* The loftiest kind is that of the highest imagination—and, for this reason only, 'Ligeia' may be called my *best* tale." H. E. Belden, in "Poe's Criticism of Hawthorne," *Anglia,* 1900, XXIII, 376-404, has convincingly demonstrated that Hawthorne's manner had little in common with Tieck's, except with one of Tieck's stories, but that earlier critics in England and America had suggested a similarity, and that Poe was sincere but mistaken in believing that Hawthorne had imitated Tieck. In "A Fable for Critics," Lowell called Hawthorne "a Puritan Tieck."

[31] *Works,* XI, 102-13. Poe thought that in at least one respect the tale had a point of superiority over the poem (108-09): "In fact, while the *rhythm* of this latter is an essential aid in the development of the poet's highest idea—the idea of the Beautiful—the artificialities of this rhythm are an inseparable bar to the development of all points of thought or expression which have their basis in *Truth.* But Truth is often, and in very great degree, the aim of the tale. Some of the finest tales are tales of ratiocination. Thus the field of this species of composition, if not in so elevated a region on the mountain of Mind, is a table-land of far vaster extent than the domain of the mere poem. Its products are never so rich, but infinitely more numerous, and more appreciable by the mass of mankind. The writer of the prose tale, in short, may bring to his theme a vast variety of modes or inflections of thought and expression— (the ratiocinative, for example, the sarcastic, or the humorous) which are not only antagonistical to the nature of the poem, but absolutely forbidden by one of its most peculiar and indispensable adjuncts; we allude, of course, to rhythm. It may be added here, *par parenthèse,* that the author who aims at the purely beautiful in a prose tale is laboring at great disad-

vantage. For Beauty can be better treated in the poem. Not so with terror, or passion, or horror, or a multitude of such other points."
[32]*Works*, XI, 108; XIII, 152-53.

III. POE ON POETRY

[1]See Floyd Stovall, "Poe's Debt to Coleridge," University of Texas *Studies in English*, X, 70-127, for an excellent discussion.

[2]*Works*, 85-91. The perfunctory notice included in *Works*, VIII, 1-2, from *SLM*, January, 1835, is almost certainly not by Poe. In XIII, 125-41 (published in *Godey's Lady's Book*, April, 1846), he admitted that he had under-valued Bryant because of his "elegancies and accuracies," but no one realized that critics had been beguiled into a popular error: "It will never do to claim for Bryant a genius of the loftiest order, but there has been latterly, since the days of Mr. Longfellow and Mr. Lowell, a growing disposition to deny him *genius* in *any* respect. He is now commonly spoken of as 'a man of high poetical *talent*, very *'correct,'* with a warm appreciation of the beauty of nature and great descriptive powers, but rather too much of the old-school manner of Cowper, Goldsmith and Young.' This is the truth, but not the whole truth. Mr. Bryant has genius, and that of a marked character, but it has been overlooked by modern schools, because deficient in those externals which have become in measure symbolical of those schools."

[3]*Works*, VIII, 275-318. The books were *The Culprit Fay, and other Poems*, by Drake, and *Alnwick Castle, with other Poems*, by Halleck. Quotations on 282-83, 284-85, 296.

[4]*Works*, VIII, 275-318, especially 300, 302, 309, and 317-18.

[5]*Works*, VIII, 122-42, especially 124-26. In the same article he also reviewed rather favorably books by Miss H. F. Gould and Mrs. E. F. Ellet. For his appreciation of Mrs. Hemans as author and as person, see IX, 195-204. On Chivers, see *Works*, XII, 201-206; XV, 241-42. The quotation on Mrs. Smith's work is in XIII, 86.

[6]*Works*, XIV, 153; X, 41; XVI, 137. In "Landor's Cottage," the domain "struck me with the keenest sense of combined novelty and propriety—in a word, of *poetry*."

[7]A review of Thomas Moore's *Alciphron*, *Works*, X, 60-71. Poe here called "The Culprit Fay" a "puerile abortion" belonging to the "class of the pseudo-ideal" (62). Poe listed a few works that he thought imaginative, suggestive, and mystic: "The 'Prometheus Vinctus' of Aeschylus; the 'Inferno' of Dante; the 'Destruction of Numantia' by Cervantes; the 'Comus' of Milton; the 'Ancient Mariner,' the 'Christabel' and the 'Kubla Khan' of Coleridge; the 'Nightingale' of Keats; and most especially, the 'Sensitive Plant' of Shelley and the 'Undine' of De La Motte Fouqué. These two latter poems (for we call them both such) are the finest possible examples of the purely *ideal*. There is little of fancy here, and everything of imagination."

[8]*Works*, XI, 68-85; quotations 73, 70-71, 75-76. Poe thought poorly of American satirical verse (XII, 107; XIII, 165-68), and that humor and poetry were related only when each was presented in rhythm and rhyme (X, 24): "Thus the only bonds between humorous verse and poetry,

properly so called, is that they employ in common a certain tool." Reviewing Longfellow's *Ballads and Other Poems* (*Works*, XI, 69-85), Poe made one of his most trenchant distinctions between art and literal truth: "That the chief merit of a picture is its *truth*, is an assertion deplorably erroneous. Even in Painting, which is, more essentially than Poetry, a mimetic art, the proposition cannot be sustained. Truth is not even *the aim*. Indeed it is curious to observe how very slight a degree of truth is sufficient to satisfy the mind, which acquiesces in the absence of numerous essentials in the thing depicted. . . . If truth is the highest aim of either Painting or Poesy, then Jan Steen was a greater artist than Angelo, and Crabbe is a more noble poet than Milton." Yet he also declared flatly, in *Eureka*, that "Poetry and Truth are one."

9*Works*, XI, 243-49; XIII, 165-75.

10*Works*, XIV, 193-208. Norman Foerster, in his usually perceptive essay on Poe in *American Criticism*, seemingly misunderstood completely what Poe wrote (12-13); W. C. Brownell in his unsympathetic yet able essay in *American Prose Masters* (147-48) so distorted Poe's words that he could declare flatly that Poe had "an intellectual repugnance" to truth.

11*Works*, XIV, 266-92, 233; XIII, 151; XI, 268. Quotation in XIV, 267.

12*Works*, XIII, 73, 112. On 113, he added that "The truthfulness, the indispensable truthfulness of the drama, has reference only to the fidelity with which it should depict nature." It was not the purpose of fiction to inculcate truth, but to be "truthful without conveying the true." Writing to James Russell Lowell in answer to Lowell's complaint that he was unfit to write narrative, unless in a dramatic form, Poe characteristically responded: "It is not you that are unfit for the task—but the task for you—for any poet. Poetry must eschew narrative—except, as you say, dramatically. I mean to say that the *true* poetry—the highest poetry—must eschew it. The Iliad is *not* the highest. The connecting links of a narration—the frequent passages which have to serve the purpose of binding together the parts of the story, are necessarily prose, from their very explanatory nature. To color them—to gloss over their prosaic nature (for this is the most which can be done) requires great skill. Thus Byron, who was no artist, is always driven, in his narrative, to fragmentary passages, eked out with asterisks. Moore succeeds better than any one. His 'Alciphron' is wonderful in the force, grace, and nature of its purely narrative passages" (*Letters*, I, 238-39).

13*Works*, XII, 112-21; quotation on 118. He reviewed Mrs. Mowatt's *Fashion* and her acting again, XII, 184-92, especially praising her performance in *The Bride of Lammermoor*.

14*Doings of Gotham*, collected by Jacob E. Spannuth with an Introduction and Comments by Thomas Ollive Mabbott, Pottsville, Pennsylvania, 1929, 97, in a review of Robert T. Conrad's *Aylmere, or, Jack Cade*.

15*Works*, X, 66; XVI, 71-72; XII, 131-32 (where he found in Sophocles' *Antigone* "an insufferable *baldness*, or platitude, the inevitable result of inexperience in Art"). The best discussion of Poe's dramatic criticism that I have seen is Ch. II of N. B. Fagin's *The Histrionic Mr. Poe*, Baltimore, 1949. For his frequent quotations from plays, see 97-98.

16*Works*, XVI, 100; *Burton's Gentleman's Magazine*, V (Nov., 1839), 282; *Works*, XII, 211, 227; XIII, 52; Fagin, 117-18. William Hazlitt's insistence on Shakspeare's realism and trueness to life in his *The Characters of Shakspeare* was "a radical error" of interpretation in an otherwise excellent book (XII, 226-27) .

17*Works*, X, 27-30 (in 1839 he thought *Tortesa* "the best play from the pen of an American author") , XIII, 38-54; XV, 233; *Doings of Gotham*, 93-101 (in 1841 Poe thought *Aylmere* "perhaps, the best American play") ; *Works*, XII, 120; XVI, 109-10.

18*Works*, X, 67-70; XVI, 27 (here Poe qualifies his praise: Moore has "a fine taste—*as far as it goes*") ; XIV, 183. In 1841 he thought Moore "the most skillful literary artist of his day,—perhaps of any day,—a man who stands in the singular and really wonderful predicament of being undervalued on account of the profusion with which he has scattered about him his good things" (X,147) ; but in 1845 he would not admit that Moore was entitled to be called a poet of imagination: "When Moore is termed a fanciful poet, the epithet is precisely applied; he *is*. He is fanciful in 'Lalla Rookh,' and had he written the 'Inferno,' there he would have been fanciful still: for not only is he essentially fanciful, but he has no ability to be anything more, unless at rare intrevals—by snatches—and with effort" (XII, 38) .

19*Works*, X, 71-80; XII, 89-93. Harrison has grouped Poe's articles, under the title of "The Longfellow War," in XII, 41-106. C. S. Brigham, *Edgar Allan Poe's Contributions to Alexander's Weekly Magazine*, Worcester, Mass., 1943, 33-34. A thorough analysis of Poe's charges and of the countercharges by Longfellow's friends is made by Sidney P. Moss in Ch. 5 of *Poe's Literary Battles*. See also Miller, *The Raven and the Whale*, esp. 129-30 (although Miller's assumption that Poe wrote the article signed "Outis" seems unwarranted; it was probably by Cornelius C. Felton) . Perhaps the best treatment of Poe's concept of plagiarism is Nelson F. Adkins, " 'Chapter on American Cribbage': Poe and Plagiarism," *Papers of the Bibliographical Society of America*, 42: 169-210. The title was taken from that of a Poe memorandum of an article he planned to write.

20*Letters*, I, 158-59, 160-61, 187; *Works*, XV, 4, 191; XVI, 97.

21"The Poets of America," *Foreign Quarterly Review*, XXXII (Jan., 1844) , 291-324. *Letters*, I, 246-47. See Moss, 157-58, for Lowell's letter. New York *Evening Mirror*, Jan. 13, 14, 1845; reprinted Jan. 25, 1845.

22R. B. Shuman, "Longfellow, Poe, and the *Waif*," *PMLA*, LXXVI (March, 1961) , 155-56. New York *Evening Mirror*, Jan. 20, 1845. Buffalo *Western Literary Messenger*, Jan. 25, 1845. See Moss, 159-65, 169. *Evening Mirror*, Feb. 5, 1845; reprinted in *Weekly Mirror*, Feb. 8, 1845; *Evening Mirror*, Feb. 15, 1845; reprinted in *Weekly Mirror*, Feb. 22, 1845; *Evening Mirror*, March 1, 1845; *Broadway Journal*, I (March 8, 1845) , 159. It seems to have been Mary E. Phillips, *Edgar Allan Poe—The Man*, Chicago, 1926, II, 956 ff., who was most convinced that the Outis article was written by Poe. Her argument was refuted by Killis Campbell in "Who Was Outis?", University of Texas *Studies in English*, 1928, VIII, 107-09. I see little reason to doubt that Felton was Outis.

23*Works*, XII, 41-106; the significant quotations are on 70-71, 78-79, 86, 103, 105-06.

²⁴On Coleridge, *Works*, VIII, xxxv-xliii; IX, 51-52; XI, 255-56. See Floyd Stovall, "Poe's Debt to Coleridge," University of Texas *Studies in English*, X, 70-127. On Shelley, *Works*, VIII, 283; quotation on XII, 32, and XVI, 148. On Keats, XI, 76, Poe declared that Keats is "the sole British poet who has never erred in his themes. Beauty is always his aim." In *Letters*, I, 257-58, he wrote to Lowell: "I am profoundly excited by music, and by some poems—those of Tennyson especially—whom, with Keats, Shelley, Coleridge (occasionally) and a few others of like thought and expression, I regard as the *sole* poets." He told Chivers that he regarded Keats as "the greatest of the English Poets of the same age, if not at any age . . . . He was far in advance of the best of them, with the exception of Shelley, in the study of his themes. His principal fault is the grotesqueness of his abandon." Of Shelley he said that "In passion he was supreme, but it was an unfettered enthusiasm ungoverned by the amenities of Art . . . . His principal forte was powerful abandon of rhythmical conception . . . . But he lacked just that Tennysonian Art necessary to the creation of a perfect Poem" (Chivers' *Life of Poe*, 46-48) .

²⁵*Works*, XII, 33-35, 180; XVI, 28-30, 150; XIV, 289; Chivers' *Life of Poe*, 47. Poe's 1842 review of *The Poems of Alfred Tennyson* (*Works*, XI, 127-31) was decidedly moderate: "That Tennyson has genius cannot be denied, but his works have too little of many qualities, especially of manliness, to be long popular. We have better poets at home, Bryant, Longfellow, and others." See the index to John Olin Eidson's *Tennyson in America*, Athens, Georgia, 1943, and esp. pp. 42-45.

²⁶*Works*, XII, 1-35; XIII, 200-01; XIV, 182; XVI, 135-36. Poe told Chivers (*Life of Poe*, 40) that she stood, "when compared with the male Poets of England, midway between Shelley and Tennyson—possessing more of the Shelleyan abandon than the truly Tennysonian Poetic sense— but infinitely above any female that England ever produced—or, in fact, any other Country." He was flattered by her praise of his work; see *Letters*, II, 319-20, 329, 336.

²⁷*Letters*, I, 78; *Works*, XIV, 209-65; XVI, 84-86. In "Marginalia," XVI, 137, Poe wrote that "the sentiments deducible from the conception of sweet sound simply, are out of the reach of analysis—although referable, possibly, in their last result, to that merely mathematical recognition of *equality* which seems to be *the root of all Beauty*."

²⁸*Works*, XIV, 193-208. Ravel's statement is quoted in Fagin, 146 n.

²⁹*Works*, XIV, 275-76.

A SUMMING UP

¹*Works*, XI, 131; XII, 146, 155.

²*Works*, XIII, 17 86, 125, 217-18.

³*Works*, XI, 112-13. Poe may also have been hurt by Hawthorne's 1843 comment in Lowell's *Pioneer* that "Mr. Poe had gained ready admittance for the sake of his imagination, but was theatened with ejectment, as belonging to the obnoxious class of critics."

Index

109